D1235993

MAYBE
GOD
WAS BUSY

A Memoir

JULIE MARIE MANSFIELD

For information address
Walk A Mile Publishing, LLC,
4582 NE Second Avenue, Miami, FL 33137.

ISBN: 061581476X

ISBN 13: 9780615814766

Names have been changed to protect only the innocent.
Embellishments Forgone.

ACKNOWLEDGEMENTS

My eternal gratitude for the many men in my life; without whom I would not have had this story to tell.

Special thanks for all those who encouraged me to write. Dryfoot, you *made* sure I wrote. Claude you are my rock. And to my girls Jenee and Fabienne, thanks for your love and your patience in me finding me—and I cherish you for telling me, "your abuse doesn't define you, Mom."

To the Journey Institute, you have given me my life, and for that words are simply not enough though to you I say, 'thank you for caring.'

To those of my cousins who have suffered the unspeakable ravages of sex abuse, I stand with you knowing all too well the evils placed on you. I offer my love, my support, my empathy.

Cascia, my siblings, Angie B, Jason, Bernard, Garfield, Granville, Suzan, Honorebel: much love for your unwavering support. Ray, thank you seems so empty, yet that's all I can say.

My Uncle, thanks for being my lifeboat. Auntie Winsome thanks for help leading the charge to help us heal. My other uncles Buzz, Verdel and David: thank you for being amazingly decent uncles.

For all the girls and boys altered by sex abuse: it is not a death sentence. If I didn't die, you have every reason to live, free from guilt, free from shame. You have done absolutely nothing wrong, nothing to have to carry the burden of your offender's shame.

To all others, thanks for the support, expressed or implied. It's fuel for my soul for the work ahead as we look to reclaim my beloved Jamaica from the predators that lay in wait.

To my abusers: Though you have touched the body, you simply could not destroy my soul—and it is that soul that has made me Julie Marie Mansfield…irrepressible.

Dear God,

I cannot understand why he always wants to hug,
Wants to touch
It is really hard to believe it is as he says,
Because he loves me so much.
I tell him it makes me feel dirty,
But he just grins and moans
When he says I should act a little flirty.
So now when he tries to get me alone,
I just quiet my heart and will my little feet
To run far, far away from home.
But truth is I don't know exactly what to do,
Cause I am so afraid for my sisters
And my brothers too.
I wish my mother could open her eyes
A little wider so she can see,
Why he prefers, not her, but my little siblings and me.
A child of his loin, pain from her groin,
Who cares to live when to the pain I am conjoined?
Here I am Lord, just turned six,
Should I not be playing with shadows; picking up sticks?
Instead I am confused by love, shackled by fear
So burdened by shame
And all they want is to sacrifice me
To keep intact their family name.
But one day soon when I am a mother,
With my kids I will trust no one
Not even my own brother.
Until then I hope you will try a little harder
To shield us from them
From all the evil that lives in the souls of your men.

*Truly, I say to you, today you will
be with me in paradise.*

—Luke 23:43

Yes, per square mile, Jamaica has more churches
than any other nation——in the world.

Yes, per capita, Jamaica has had the highest
murder rate——in the world.

❧

Another thunder, muffled by the greenery, as a fisherman fells a tree. He shapes the timber into a boat, armed with only an adze and patient determination. It could be the coast off the jungles of Africa but it's a remote forest in Jamaica, deep in St. Thomas, one of those parishes where women go to church in sun-bathed cotton dresses that lay in moth-laden drawers, awaiting that Sunday trip to Church, the highlight of the social week.

It is a week punctuated by days that start when the rooster crows, signaling a procession of the day's errands: sweeping wood floors; polishing bare ochre-stained tiles with wax and a coconut brush; cooking at noon for dinner at six; hanging hand-washed clothes for the sun to dry. Only afterwards do neighbors visit neighbors—ambling down earth paths in the dappled sunlight between trees, where hummingbirds dart, butterflies float, and tropical birds call out. Neighbors sit impassively with neighbors, communicating through long silences. Warm beer, or stout, and a cigarette or two help ease afternoons into evenings.

While adults sit in company, teenagers take to any local beach, mostly on foot; no roads, no cars, no motors, and the quiet is interrupted only when waves, deliberately and with violent intent, crash into rocks. It is usually a beach where coconut trees shaped by years of coastal coercion are bent just enough for seating and natural shade and where fishermen launch their boats before sunrise and then cook their catch, just before sunset.

Then it's back home to the houses of sun-baked timber or rendered stone and brick, crafted by neighbors with no training or money—just the good sense to be neighborly. Where yards, even dirt ones, are free from leaves just fallen, and where verandahs so easy, so relaxed, beckon you from afar.

It is all so unequivocally tropical, paradise in its original sense. Primal you could say.

There's something about living in houses with no air conditioning needed; something about the smell of rain meeting the dry dirt; something about homemade boats pulled up on the beach and tied to coconut trees; something about being lulled to sleep by the pitter-patter of rain on a galvanized metal roof; something about the warm breeze suffusing your whole being with a comforting caress. Something about everyday Jamaica, the island paradise that Christopher Columbus said was "the fairest island eyes have beheld; mountainous and the land seems to touch the sky."

I imagine it's the Jamaica millions of tourists seek but fail to find behind sky-high concrete walls meant to keep everyday Jamaicans at bay. For visitors adventurous enough to venture beyond the tourist veil, my Jamaica has a way of endearing itself, making believers out of doubters and turning even pimps into preachers. Long before Bob Marley became synonymous with Reggae and Reggae became synonymous with Jamaica, other ambassadors included Errol Flynn, Noel Coward, Ian Fleming.

While this is no pulpit, it would be un-Jamaican of me not to brag about my island, barely bigger than a football field yet the third largest island in the Caribbean—largest English speaking, tank yuh. And yes, we speak English, not Henlgish. Confession: we had to practice the devil out of our hs...

Like having to recite, everyday before school: *"Harry went to Hampstead, Harry lost His Hat, Harry's mother said to Harry, Harry where's your Hat."* Let's tek a stroll down memory lane, but put on you comfy shoes, it's a rocky road.

⤙

At Seaforth Primary School one thing was certain, we'd be subject to some fat teacher's admonition, the worst of which came from Mrs. Hutchinson who was not only fat but yellow too. Of course, it was entirely possible we hated her because of her translucent yellow skin. Even among the mix of mutts (Chinese + Indian; French + African; Scottish + German with a tinge of Indian or African) she was an anomaly. We would have downright loathed her if she had the hair to match to skin, but lucky for us she had hair like the steel wool we used to scrub pots charred by angry wood fires. Course. Kinky. Unenviable. We might not have been the lightest but at least we had hair, pretty, manageable hair. In any case, Mrs. Hutchinson's brand of pale was reason enough to hate her, and for her to think herself better than us.

Though her hair broke many a comb and devoured many a pomade, at least she wouldn't have to bathe in Ambi or Nadinola to banish the black from her skin. And who could ever forget the ridiculous glasses Mrs. Hutchinson wore. They only added to her caricature. Really, they were meant to be bathroom mirrors but in her insistence to show *she* could afford reading glasses, she strapped wire rims around them and decorated her face, pinching her nostrils into slithers through which air only narrowly escaped.

Her '*I might not have the best hair but at least I'm not a fucking blackie tutu*' demeanor made sure we know she was boss. Though I must confess: I often imagined beating the yellow off her if only she would leave the security of the thick leather strap she'd soak overnight so she could leave welts on whomever selfish enough not to have memorized the entire multiplication table. It was mandatory recitation every morning. But she was fair, I think. She gave us options: go outside and pick up 13 times 13 pebbles and hold them in your mouth for 13 minutes. Or, stand in front of the entire class of third graders—in uniform starched to a crisp and upturned looked like an umbrella on the wrong side of a gale. Frilly panties would be exposed and only the threat of their own beating would keep the rest of the class from erupting into laughter.

She pleasured herself each of the thirteen times she'd lower the strap, and had the nerve to flinch so as to escape the splatter of blood when belt and bottom collided. See, welts would invariably part and send streams of blood from backside to thigh to calf to ankle to floor, free to mingle with the fresh piss that had just escaped the bladder. But there must have been something to all that beating, blood and urine. All these years later I can tell you thirteen times thirteen equals 169; without checking fingers and toes, or worse, consulting a calculator or pebbles.

Anyway, I digressed. I was telling you about my everyday Jamaica, and how we gave the world, even if my the most circuitous means, Colin Powell, Alicia Keyes, Harry Belafonte, Naomi Campbell, Louis Farrakhan, Marcus Garvey, Bob Marley, Lennox Lewis, Osafa Powell, Barrington Irving, Usain Bolt, Heavy D... And that's a truncated list.

We know how to stake a claim to success and before long we'll find a way to make President Obama "Jamaican." We also know how to shun disgrace. Canada can keep Ben Johnson. Yes indeed, as old time people used to say, "wi likkle but wi tallawah." Yes English.

Meaning: We are small but mighty.

David slew Goliath, didn't he?

✝ ✝ ✝

And it came to pass, when they had brought them forth abroad, that he said, escape for thy life; look not behind thee, neither stay thou in all the plain; Escape to the mountain, lest thou be consumed.

—Genesis 19:17

Recollections of an idyllic childhood make for a very buoyant life vest. And say what you will, looking back doesn't keep me from moving forward. How can I know where I'm going, and how to get there, if I don't know where I've been? Clichés are clichés for a reason.

I remember being 6 years old and laying in the no-name river that offered its residents—and visitors no privacy. We could see clear through, watching every janga (shrimp) and fish and eel and suckie and crayfish go about their daily business of surviving. And though they tried their best to seek the shelter of a rock, we would take joy in evicting them to watch the scurry to find other havens. Best by far was when they'd mistake our traps, our bare hands cupped and waiting to capture them for our all-in-one pot.

Yes, we'd actually had a pot on the wood fire, waiting, and in would go everything we could possibly find: bananas, yam, cocoa, rice, eggs, fresh catch, thyme, salt, black pepper—everything. Sometimes it tasted like heaven, sometimes it tasted like I imagined the food in hell. No matter, it satisfied our hunger, and often our greed.

Then there were the days, mostly Fridays, when lead by Dee, our mother, we'd form a gaggle from Seaforth to Spring. All five miles on foot, and singing songs of praises, accompanied by the jingle of Dee's tambourine and clapping of our hands.

Singing was interrupted by mangoes too ripe to ignore tempting Dee to put the tambourine aside long enough to extend her reach, often without stretching, to pick an East Indian or Julie mango. We didn't care for Common mangoes. They were, well, common. There was no need to wash, not even a wipe; they went from tree to mouth.

A fresh-picked mango leaf funneled water from a spring to satisfy the thirst. Yes, fresh fruits and real spring water! No wonder we looked forward to trailing our tambourine-toting mother.

So you see, I have good reasons to look back, on a child-hood most idyllic. Now here is the problem. Idyllic yes. Ideal? Not even close. It wasn't all about the miles of white sand beaches, to-die-for-weather, broad smiles and no worries mon.

For me there was too much to worry about, especially the men in my life, the men in my family. Besides, I don't want to be burdened by selective memory. If I am to properly clear the clutter in my mind, I must recall the good and the not so good. Such a task cannot be undertaken with filters, just one reason I've opted to remove them on my recollection for a while now, enabling me to go through the dark days, long nights, uneasy silence and sinful secrets that plagued *my* everyday Jamaica.

⸺

I've been burying and hiding and molding and protecting for decades, you could say to keep some of the evils of my childhood from completely consuming me. Had it not been for miraculously detaching, I suppose it's not hard to imagine me a cliché, you know, product of the sustained sexual abuse meant to direct my life: prostitution, drug addiction, promiscuity, alcoholism, death, etc. Luckily I've always been stubborn, too hard headed to follow the script; too competitive to have even chronic childhood sex abuse and incest dictate my outcome. Not that I haven't traded some soul, sometimes even consciously mind you. Sometimes it feels I have none left to trade, like there is nothing to give, actually, less than nothing. I sometimes flirt with life in the red, owing too many people bits of me. Worse, I don't know when these debts will be repaid, not that I ever really promised to repay.

Even the devil knows a promise is of comfort to a fool. Adages are adages for a reason. Have you heard the one about the rabbit never weighing more than its quarter? Well, looks like my quarter is up. Unlike those of the men who promised to care, who promised to love, who promised to protect. The only loving and protecting they were doing were of themselves and their dirty little urges.

But as my grandma used to say, if you want to know the source, you have to go to the head of the river. So let me start at the beginning, with the beginning, back to the everyday Jamaica that lured the likes of Elizabeth Taylor, Peter O'Toole, Errol Flynn, Noel Coward and Ian Fleming to take refuge in a paradise unspoiled by modern advances. There were other advances—unwanted, pervasive and sinister; advances that entombed me in paradise, I imagine not unlike the caterpillars

we would confine to glass bottles so we could watch them turn
into butterflies.

$\backsim$

I was 'big' for 8. Not fat, big. In fact, I don't think I've grown
up any, maybe out a little, but not up. I think I might have been
born 5'8". I was what they called mawga, so skinny my dress
would drape like it had been hitched on a nail on the back of the
door, and flat like bammy, the Jamaican cousin to pita bread.

If it weren't for my big head, I'd be almost invisible. I was
saved by my big head, topped only by bigger hair, "pretty hair."
Though I was mawga, at least I was fair, unlike those other
kids with noses stretched from ear to ear. I had a straight,
pretty likkle nose. And even at the youngest age, I knew my
times table past the 13 times 13 with which most teenagers still
struggled. I never understood why they couldn't just sing their
times table: two ones two, two twos four, two fours eight,
etc. Coupling the singsong with hopscotch or jump rope or
marbles made for hours of play anyway. Singsong also helped
ease us into familiarity on the trips to see Pops and Mama, my
mother's parents. Everyone called them Pops and Mama. Only
the truly formal called them Bredda D and Sista Montgomery.

Pops and Mama lived in a mega house in the Blue Mountains
of St. Thomas; so far in the hills their nearest neighbor was a
good three miles in any direction. The view was surreal in its
beauty—coconut trees raced with breadfruit trees to reach the
sun.

The sounds of natural waterfalls lulled. The smell of fresh
air was, well, fresh. And the frolicking of blue jays, cardinals,

humming birds and butterflies was free entertainment. The cool of the Blue Mountain seemed to tame the violence prone Jamaican sun. It might have explained why that part of St. Thomas always seemed cooler than the rest. It was all at once serene and surreal.

✝ ✝ ✝

*You say, 'I am rich; I have acquired wealth and do
not need a thing.' But you do not realize that you
are wretched, pitiful, poor, blind and naked.
I counsel you to buy from me gold refined in the
fire, so you can become rich; and white clothes to
wear, so you can cover your shameful nakedness;
and salve to put on your eyes, so you can see.*

—Revelation 3:17-18

Pops, born Trevor Montgomery, was the son of a Scottish mother and black father. My grandfather was a man of stature, dignified. He was a pastor. No, he was an Overseer because he was in charge of at least four churches in two parishes, Portland and St. Thomas. 'A pastor only leads one church at a time.' Besides, when he did work, he was a supervisor at Serge, then the primary if not sole employer of able-bodied men, and of mothers of fatherless children. His reign at Serge didn't last long though. He started his own sugar plantation and that made the scores of people he employed revere him.

Pops was flashy though he swore was a servant of God and as such had to carry himself in a manner pleasing his Father. His hair was always made to rest under the top part of my grandmother's hosiery turned head cap, so that it would be extra wavy, showing off his 'good hair' thanks to his biracial genes. He always wore a suit; NEVER EVER jeans or god forbid shorts even on those days the few paved roads would literally melt. Pops was always crowned by a fedora, tilted just right with a certain deliberateness to hide the fact that he had tried scores of positions before settling on the one the said, 'I'm not trying too hard.'

Come Sunday, the most sacred of church days, he always wore a three-piece suit adorned with a pocket square, his Sunday-only fedora and just-polished shoes. Perhaps his most prized possession was the crocodile attaché that housed his bible, handkerchief and a few icy mints.

Cars completed my grandfather. He always had one of the 10 or so cars in our district. I remember his red pickup truck, his white Cortina and his orange car with no name. Despite living out loud through the obvious symbols of success, my grandfather always maintained he was a humble servant of the Lord and as such he had to conduct himself in a manner pleasing of his Boss. I guess his Boss commissioned the house with its 10 bedrooms, formal living room, formal dining room and all the trappings that identified the abode as that of a servant of the Lord. Most everyone around lived in weathered wooden shacks with broom-swept dirt floors.

Pops, duly anointed King of Spring, perched his house at the very pinnacle of the hill, affording panoramic views of the valleys and streams and rivers encompassing his domain. The house, nestled in the bosom of the Blue Mountains, sat in watch of backs curled and 'leatherized' by the too-hot-to-breathe sun, hurling machetes at the sugarcane as though each reed threatened their 'manhood.'

We were never sure what engendered the omnipresent whisper "Wha mek dem a fi mek such a big house if nearly all a di pickney dem already grown and gawn?"

Translation: Why do they need such a big house if nearly all the kids are grown and gone?"

Meaning: They think they're better than us because Pops had a white mother and Mama had a half white father. That made them look—and acted different—from most other folks.

My grandparents often regaled us with stories of their "envied" lineage. Pops' mother, Nana, had hair so long she had to put her braids on her lap to avoid sitting on them. And she had eyes as blue as seawater. Mama, born Edna Perrier, was herself a mulatto thanks to French father and black mother. She always dressed to Pops' approval; she was a reflection of him in every pertinent way. Whether deliberately or not being able to maintain his gait, she always walked a few paces behind him, and she only ever referred to him as pastor. Not Trevor, his given name. Not Pops. Pastor. Not even after bearing 14 children. I often wondered what comprised quiet conversations between them. Perhaps strangest still, I have never heard her call him directly. Instead, she'd wait until she was within hearing and would say something like, "you know," or "but tell me something."

Mama was rigid in her routine: laundry by hand on Monday; iron everything, including dish towels, sheets and underwear on Tuesday; clean the entire house on Wednesday, etc.

We loved our grandparents, loved being in their company. We especially enjoyed the challenge of braiding Pops' hair. We were in absolute heaven when he would just sit there, eyes closed, whistling as we played about in his hair. But like a lot of the kids around, his hair was unruly and completely disobedient; it was slippery and uncooperative. Eventually we figured out it would take at least two people: one to plait and one to hold so it wouldn't immediately unravel upon release. We were intrigued and proud.

He was our grandfather with the big house and the cars
and the green eyes and the fancy clothes and the employees and
the respect and the wife with the French maiden name and the
pretty pickney dem. Yes, he was ours and we were his as long
as we didn't do anything to cause him to "hold his head" down.
Like us girls wearing shorts or pants or straightening our hair
or wearing jewelry or talking to boys or wearing makeup
or perhaps most mortal: not going to Church Sunday morning, Sunday afternoon, Sunday night, Monday night, Tuesday
night, Wednesday night, Thursday night, Friday night and yes,
Saturday night.

Pops hated even the mere mention of his sons wanting to
grow dreadlocks or talking to people with dreadlocks. It wasn't
even worth thinking one of his girls might be so inclined to
grow locks; that was unheard of for women to want to engage
in such rebellious devil-worshipping shenanigans. He hated
dem "dutty rasta."

Like hundreds of times before, we arrived at our Pops' house
before 'cock crow.' The morning sun had just started searing
the dew, and we were never quite sure what most intrigued us:
the fog snaking its way back to the sky, critters greeting one
another, or the flitter of hummingbirds darting as if still blind
by the darkness of night.

Stephen and George, my two youngest uncles born a year
apart on 9/11, had already used coconut brushes to remove
the prior day's evidence of life from red-ochre floors while
Mama made porridge, fried dumplings and ackee & salt fish

for breakfast. My uncles had maneuvered their way and were standing like vultures-in-waiting behind Pops in his mahogany chair behind his mahogany table, waiting for him to finish picking at his breakfast so they could devour the leftovers. But as soon as Pops saw me, he called me over with a toss of his head and handed me his plate of barely-touched fried dumplings and ackee & salt fish.

I wasn't surprised because he always told everyone I was his favorite gran pickney. You can imagine this brought out the expected in Stephen and George. Yes, they were teenage boys, typical of the time and place, and doing typical teenage things for the time and place.

Blind to the virtues of school, they had both simply stopped attending; they simply couldn't see what the hell school had to offer them. They both knew far more than Pops and Mama—combined, and both preferred partying to praying. Stephen and George shared lots of things and times: they religiously hunted birds with homemade slingshots, they preferred JC Lodge to Jesus Christ, and they took delight in torturing us, though as fate would have it, one tortured me far more than the other.

One would tell me he liked me so much he thinks he loves me; the other said nothing but tried to show his affections. You could say it was a rather dysfunctional game of show and tell.

✝ ✝ ✝

None of you shall approach to any of that is near
of kin to him,
To uncover their nakedness; I am the Lord.

—Leviticus 18:6

was giddy with excitement when, just after breakfast, George asked if I wanted to go visit Junior, *his* brother but *my* favorite uncle, who lived 30 minutes by foot, a bit quicker on even a rickety bicycle up for the mostly downhill trip. My mother had said I could go but only if I was back before the sun dried her spit. I could see why she wanted me back, to get Pops' barely-touched Southern fried chicken and rice & peas she was busy preparing for that evening's dinner.

Why had George invited me and not my brothers and sisters or cousins? I was Pops' favorite so I must have been George's as well. It wasn't hard to imagine that, he was less than a decade my senior. In fact, my oldest brother Oin was months older than George. My uncle and I could easily have been siblings. But if I was big for my age, George was gargantuan, he was every bit the big uncle. Not fat, just big. I imagined it was all the intramural competitive cross-country sports in which he had participated while still in school, most if not always with an irrefutable win.

As big as he was though, George was a bit lazy, typical of his time and place, and preferred riding his bicycle reconstituted from other bicycles. I didn't mind even though I knew we had to push it back, up hill. I sat sideways on the crossbar and giggled as we went over the bumps in the mostly dirt road, most of the asphalt had long succumbed to incessant flooding and no maintenance.

The sounds of pebbles popping under the wheels were melodic, musical. I giggled even more as we leaned in and out of the 'esses' that gave the one-lane mostly dirt road all the characteristics of a good country road. George did his best to stay in the middle and avoid the sugarcane leaves slapping us as that encounter would most definitely cause cuts if not gashes, depending on whether we were going into or coming out of an 'ess.'

I tried to count how many coconut trees towered above breadfruit trees, which towered above mango trees, which towered above the cane. I tried to count the number of but-terflies fluttering, the number of birds signing, the number of hummingbirds darting. Futile. I was giggling way too much, besides it's not easy to concentrate and count when you're con-stantly interrupted by thought of 'are we there yet.'

I wasn't sure how much time had passed since we left Pops', or if indeed my mother's spit had dried. If pressed though I could tell you exactly how many pebbles popped at the command of the bicycle. The big bend was finally in sight. The excitement grew because I knew we would lean into it, as a professional motorcycle racer, with his knee kissing the ground. I knew the precise moment I would lift my legs.

It wasn't to be.

All that rehearsal was for nothing. Out of nowhere, George dashed my hopes of leaning in and out of the damn bend. I was disappointed, and if his announcement that we couldn't take the shortcut sounded rehearsed, my response must have been appropriate.

"How yuh mean wi a tek di shawt cut?"

Translation: "What do you mean we are taking the short cut?"

Meaning: Short cut to what life-altering evil?

✝ ✝ ✝

*The nakedness of this sons' daughter,
or of thy daughter's daughter, even
their nakedness thou shalt not uncover:
for theirs is thine own nakedness.*

—Leviticus 18:10

Townsfolk swore the big bend hid tales of evil, sinister secrets, partly because you could never see what or who was on the other side. They were equally sure the short cut, hardened under the footsteps of people trying to avoid the unknown of the bend, held its own secrets. The occasional car, about one a day, way too wide to navigate the snaky shortcut had no choice by to disrupt the quiet of the bend. We had choices.

With his right foot on the back tire, George slowed the bicycle enough for me to jump off the crossbar, and with history as my teacher, I didn't just jump and stop, I jogged a bit before coming to a complete stop. That prevented me from falling over and hurting myself.

Still giggling, I started skipping, trying to determine whether the sounds I heard were coming from a cricket or a toad. Mangoes teemed with maggots and flies emitted a smell both sweet and stale. I wasn't sure if I was being caressed or inveigled by the shroud of vines. Either way, I knew I had to watch out for nettles. Last time I had nettles in my eyes, my mother had to mix water and sugar into thick syrup that she then spat into my eyes, turning burn into bearable.

George interrupted my skipping with bad news: "Di shawt cut definitely block." Strange, we were about midway along the footpath. Hmmm, a bit odd for a path used daily. There were no hurricanes; not even so much as a strong storm to have forced defenseless branches to the ground. He put the bike down on its side, the wheels still spinning violently as if to protest or warn of what was to come. Suddenly, the veil that was earlier flirting with me began threatening, sneering, almost as if it had already known something I was about to discover. I swore they instantly grew tentacles and teeth—sharp, pointy little teeth that just wanted to get their grips into me. The crickets or toads or whatever fell silent, obeying a curtain call and preparing for the show to begin. Even the sun hid. The bicycle wheels finally rested. I was glad when George finally came back from checking to ensure the path was indeed blocked.

With his return I knew the veil would soon be forced to be nice again. My uncle said we *would* have to turn back and endure the evils of the bend after all. Oh well, at least that's better than silent crickets or toads too afraid to sing, and a sun too scared to show its face.

The veils, rather than retreat, simply snickered and sneered even more and in that moment I knew enough to be more scared of my uncle that threatening bushes. George bent over as if to set the bicycle upright but instead grabbed my hand and told me to lie down. My bowels quivered and a voice deep inside whispered, no. My brain tried to cajole my feet into running but they weren't to be budged. My feet were more like unruly teenagers than feet; they weren't listening. Besides, where was I to run? To whom would I call for help? My heart pounded so violently I thought my chest would cave in and release me to the big bend.

George's hand dwarfed my right wrist that just went limp under his crush. He told me to be quiet. "Shet yuh mout nuh." He was now fully lowered onto me; his right hand now telling both my hands there was no use fighting. His left hand tried to yank my dress up and my panties down, almost in one fluid motion. I tried to kick but my legs were dead under his weight. I tried to scream but sound was lost. George stopped struggling with my dress and panties; he was undoing his zipper, all the while tightening the grip on my wrist. His head swung from side to side, up and down, like a wild horse rejecting efforts to tame it.

I wasn't sure exactly what was going to happen, but I was sure I *was* terrified of my mother's brother. I struggled, I begged, I pleaded, I made deals with God, I made deals with the devil. I promised to be good. I struggled some more. But George was a lot stronger than I, an eight-year-old twig of a girl who hated porridge even if it promised incontrovertible guard against ills. He was more than twice my size and had always eaten all his porridge and most times, Pops' barely-touched.

Even a blind man could have surmised that George had carefully planned his attack; he had known his intentions all along but had neglected to tell me, to gauge my willingness to participate in his incestuous scheme. He hadn't bothered to ask if I even knew what sex was, or if I was interested in learning from him, brother of my mother.

⟿

The leaves retracted the menace and the veil started caressing again. Only by then, I knew they weren't to be trusted. The sun came out again and the crickets or toads or whatever started their nonsense again too. Feet familiar with the path pounded the snaky earth-brown dirt that had not seen rain in quite some time. As each step nears, George hurried to put his penis with the 'white stuff coming out of it' back in his pants. (Years later, when I was old enough, I learned that 'white stuff' had a name: semen.)

He told me to be quiet and not to talk to the people to whom the approaching feet belong. He curved his back and eased himself back, allowing his penis to settle back in without betrayal or show signs of his transgression. I tried to ask the approaching feet for help, but they couldn't hear me and continued to walk by, slowing down only enough to tell George that he had just passed Junior who was walking to Pops'. George told the feet he had trouble with the bicycle, and that the chain had slipped off. He said I was crying because he had to leave me to get a piece of twig to slip the chain back on so as to not get pesky grease on his hands. I wanted to tell the approaching feet George was lying. I wanted to ask them if what he said was true, why my dress would be torn and dirty, why was I bleeding? But they just walked off and left me with my uncle. Junior had by then arrived where the bicycle once again stood upright. He wiped the tears from my face with his bare hands roughened by years of farming, tree cutting, construction, rock gathering; whatever provided money for things he might have needed, things the land didn't yield. It didn't take a genius to figure out that Junior as well as the approaching feet had just entered the path George had claimed was blocked.

"What happen to yuh baby girl?" Junior asked, using his fingers to lift my gaze from the ground. He knew something was wrong or I wouldn't have been crying. As far as he was concerned though, whatever the wrong, I was with George who would not have been the source of my tears, they were brothers, judged by each other's actions and character. If Junior would sooner die than be tempted to fuck his niece or any other family member, why should he have thought the same possible of his own brother, borne to the same mother and father.

"Neckle sting me," I lied to one uncle to protect another, and to hide my shame.

"Look out fi dem next time, dem dangerous."

"Mi know."

✝   ✝   ✝

In the shelter of your presence you hide them from the intrigues of me; in your dwelling you keep them safe from accusing tongues.

—Psalm 31:20

George's gift of $2 bought my silence. Two dollars was a lot of money in 1976. It could just about buy a year's supply of sweets. But before long I'd start to gag every time I popped a piece of busta in my mouth where George had tried to ram his seeping penis. I eventually told my mother her brother tried to ram his "thing" in my mouth and then gave me $2 to not tell anyone.

"Mi did a wonder where you get money to buy sweetie." That's all she said. Not 'are you sure? Are you okay? When did this happen? Where?' The why was obvious. Not, 'let me go see him. Let me tell the police.' Just, "Mi did a wonder where you get the money to buy so much sweetie." It was obvious she subscribed to the adage, 'Shet mout nuh ketch flies.'

Translation: A closed mouth doesn't catch flies.

Meaning: I won't stir any trouble if I say nothing. A family name in tact is worth more than a daughter's well being; you know, sacrifice the individual for the image of the clan. Message received.

I cried more than I cared; I gagged more than I giggled; I stopped eating candy, then dumplings, then just about everything. Everywhere I saw eyes, judging me, and pointy teeth snickering. I suffocated. I tried not to sleep because every time I closed my eyes I saw my uncle's penis topped with white stuff. School was both refuge and purgatory.

Did all uncles try to put their penis into the eight year-old nieces? Did all mothers fall silent? Did teachers care or were they just like uncles and mothers? Dreams turn into nightmares, weeks into months, into years, and I finally made myself forget, to stop thinking about the path and the bicycle and my introduction to the insanity of incest, of molestation.

Yes, old folks always said 'out of sight out of mind,' and even though the 'path' would often try to seep into my daily living, I had to push the path and all it meant to the nether reaches of my mind. I went back to learning, and before long I was first in my classes again. Grades three to four passed without incident. Well, insofar as I mostly made sure I was never, ever alone with George.

But no one is perfect and tried as I might, there were times when I was alone with him. And each time, he would pounce. The more he pounced, the more I buried myself into books. It was a burial that paid off, it gave me the right to go straight to grade six and skipping grade five altogether.

With the passage of time, though my ordeal was not as pervasive in my conscious, it was right to tell my mother—again. If at first you don't succeed, try, try and try again, because as they all used to say, "nothing beats failure like a good try." Besides, if I were to properly prepare for Common Entrance Exams, I needed a clear head. I was fully prepared to again be dismissed and had prepared my speech to convince. But one by one, she gathered her gaggle (me, my brother Bya, sisters

Charms & Mawma) and her tambourine. We sang, though not as enthusiastically as on previous trips. The singing was more to ease the awkwardness of us wondering why we were pulled out of school. The singing was too mechanical to be for enjoyment. Regardless, we sang. We ate fruits. We drank fresh spring water. We hop scotched over the bubbling tar.

We could smell Mama's brown stew pork from the big mango tree. If you knew Spring, the little district where my grandparents lived as well as I, you'd know you could see the house from the big mango tree. We had barely reached the front door when we heard the clacking of utensils (Pops always, always ate with a knife AND fork). But I couldn't get excited about Pops' barely-touched plate of brown stew pork, rice & peas, lettuce & tomato.

Stephen and George laid in wait.

Dee interrupted Pops picking at his food. It's hard even now to remember what was said, but I can still hear the escalated voices: Pops got loud. Dee got louder. Pops got loudest.

"But a wah dis?" asked Mama.

"Come out a mi yard," Pops bellowed as he flung his left hand motioning and reinforcing his command.

"Come pickney, come wi go a wi yard."

And with that, our trips to Spring ceased. I guess Pops didn't want to hear that his youngest child was molesting his favorite grandchild. The trek back to Seaforth seemed to have taken days. The fruits lost their luster, the spring its melody and the birds their will to fly. Even the breeze refused to whisper. Days later, Pops came to see us, but even Stevie Wonder could have seen it was no friendly let-me-pay-a-visit. With Mama in tow, Pops made his edict.

"Tell your husband him nuh Montgomery. Tell him nuh come back a mi land."

"Den how yuh mean Pops?" asked my mother, obviously buying time for her brain to process what her father had just said.

"A Montgomery land and him a Granger, so tell him nuh come back."

"Den Pops, weh him fi do bout di farm."

"Mek him go find Granger land."

"A what bring dis on Pops?"

Fin, my stepfather, walked in to see his wife and her father fully engaged, and found himself the unenviable recipient of Pops' finger pointing rage.

"Come off a mi land."

"But Bredda D a what me do you now?"

With not another word, Pops took his wife and left. The very next day, Fin's farm was flattened. Banana and plantain trees were uprooted, weeds banished, yams unearthed. The section of Pops' land that yielded Fin's bread and butter was cleared. It no longer looked like a farm but like virgin land being prepped for whatever comes next. Even the handmade crayfish traps in the stream were untied and freed to snake their course till they find their way down the river. The cows, all the cows, were tethered and beaten to death. Fin found them wound so tightly around the trees that he knew immediately they had tried desperately to flee their attackers. But apparently the more the tried to get away, the tighter the ropes got. It was obvious they completed many circles before they had completely run out of rope.

They had suffered in a message meant to tell Fin, unequivocally, "You might have married a Montgomery but that gave you no rights to other things Montgomery." And as my grandparents had long said, their boys would remain Montgomery for life, and their off springs, however gotten, would be Montgomery. Their girls, however, become products of their husbands, relieving them of the Montgomery name and its legacy.

If only it was true?

In any event, apparently I had stirred trouble by again nagging the family about a renegade uncle hell bent on inserting his penis into niece's orifices. That put a crinkle in things and rather than rebuke a wayward son, my grandparents chose to banish a complaining daughter. Just like that I had lost my grandfather. Me, my grandfather's favorite gran pickney, from whom I had received the only childhood Christmas present, the pink dress with white lacy trimming, that he had given me in front of all my siblings with ne'er an icy mint for them, had been relegated to persona non grata.

⸺ↄ

My mother had little time for hypocrisy. She was what they called 'plain.' Not plain in a homely sense because she was quite the beauty. It was hard not to mistake her for a Cherokee; cheekbones that kissed the sky, black straight-as-arrow hair she wore parted dead center. Her velvet complexion was the envy of all the women who had to choose between food and Ambi, Nadinola or whatever bleaching crème du jour. Her eyes gave almonds a run for perfection—slanted to never reveal too much. Then there were the come-hither hips. And come hither they did—men chasing her and women chasing their men chasing her. But Dee wasn't to be caught, anymore; she was snared by God. That was, after being caught at age 19 by the father her first child, a boy she named Oin; then by Paul, the father of her second son Nicholas; then by Bundy, the father of the third son Lanville. I muddled things a bit: growing up I thought Lanville's father was also *my* father, but apparently not.

So, where was I? Yea, she was called to Mumfort, my "father," before being caught by Fin, father of Bya, Stephanie and Mawma. Fin more than caught her; he cemented her marriage to the Lord through his marriage to her—or her to him. He legitimized her. She dominated him. If her upbringing and religious leanings allowed her to wear pants, hers would be bigger and bolder than her earthly husband's. Pants or no pants, she 'wore the pants in the house.' Like Pops wore the pants in his house.

We all knew not to ask questions. So we didn't ask why Oin and Lanville lived with Pops and Mama and not with us. We didn't ask why Nicholas lived with his dad way up in Font Hill where even the sole 'general store' didn't have electricity. Nor did we ask why Nicholas was the only one with light brown hair and green eyes. We were content with just Bya, Stephanie, Mawma and I living as siblings.

Bya and I were inseparable. No, his given name wasn't Bya, it was Kenton but his Indian-like hair earned him the nickname reserved for Indians, Cooly Bya, shortened to Bya. So were Mawma, given name Kansas (don't ask) and I. Stephanie, given name Dearleanne, really, really do not ask, was more often the loner and a warmonger to boot. I loved her, though she sometimes shunned love. Mawma was my favorite. I know you are probably aghast right now, damning me for admitting to a favorite. I am Jamaican; we all have favorites. Some unfavorites too!

Mawma was funny and innocent. You could see her purplish-bluish veins busy at work beneath her sickly, translucent skin. She was yellow, almost as yellow as Mrs. Hutchinson. As if at war, Mawma's hair stayed clear of her forehead, and the camel's hump permanently attached to her belly made sure the back of her dress would hang below her knees, while the front barely covered the camel's hump. She was our "wanga gut."

The source of her belly was a bit of a mystery; odd considering she wasn't particularly greedy, unlike us she didn't crave everything in sight. My baby sister was just the unfortunate owner of a 'banga gut.' Worse, the hump was exaggerated by legs too long, too wispy to belong to her—made her look like a massive tarantula that had somehow devoured a chicken. If she wasn't entirely banga gut, she was most definitely 'dry foot Addassa." Nobody knew who Addassa was, but we all imagined she had twig for legs. (If you promise not to squeal on me, I'll tell you a secret: to this day she still has the same banga gut.) And what a blabber mouth? Even our mother would say, "if me deh a road a shit and see yuh a come, mi would a siddung inna it."

Translation: If I'm shitting by the wayside and you happen to come by, I would sit it in.

Meaning: You'd never be privy to any secrets because you can't keep your mouth shut. What you know the world knows.

We suffered her mouth too. In fact, she almost wore out our mother's name: "Dee, see Julie a teef out di sugar. Dee see Bya a sneak out. Dee see Stephanie a teef out di milk. Dee see Julie a put on lipstick." Yep, what we called big mout gyal, not because her mouth was big mind you, but because she couldn't see and blind, nor could she hear and play deaf. Our threats to puncture her hump did little to quell her need to tattle. Dee would have to provide refuge for her youngest child; she had to hide Mawma between her legs, not that that would automatically stop us. We'd often reach between my mother's legs to deliver a blow to Mawma, and would only back off when Dee would ball her fist and dare us to "come, come nuh." Yes, we'd back off only then, huffing and puffing like a lion outsmarted by its prey, and despite the temper fueling that little voice that would tell us to just give her one more good biff and let all the air out of her pointy gut. To rub salt on our wounds, we had to do all the work. Clean the chimmey, wash the plates, make the bed, wash the clothes, polish the floor, fetch water, cook dinner, go to the store, iron the uniforms, sweep the yard, etc, etc. And why was Mawma the only one to call Fin 'Daddy' when we all called him Dadda? And why did we have to bathe her and brush her teeth and comb her hair and carry her on our backs. We should have deflated her hump.

But banga gut or not she was my favorite, maybe because my only other sister Stephanie was too much like my mother. Even Dee felt the competition from Stephanie and was never afraid of bringing out the claws: "gyal a mek you cantankerous so? Mawsa God, yuh fi mek some tings pass, man." But Stephanie never let anything pass. We'd all say it's because her mouth is so long. See, she sucked her thumb and that pushed her front teeth out. And no, before you ask, there was no orthodontist in Seaforth, not that anyone could've afforded such indulgencies. We were lucky to have Dentist Tony in our town of a few hundred folks.

Nobody knew exactly how many people were stuck in Seaforth. Nobody cared. Not brothers Louis and Vincent, the Chinese implants turned shopkeepers. Not Tom or his wife Miss Chin, another set of the omnipresent Chinese entrepreneurs. Not Miss Tiny or Miss Vera or Miss Puncie or the other market women. Not Downey the Bus Driver; nor Ducket the Shoemaker. Not Fin, yes our Fin, the Tailor. Not even Pops the Overseer.

Nope, nobody knew. Anyway, I was telling you about long-mouth Stephanie. Everybody, even the boys who weren't scared of anything or anyone, were scared of her, di ol' barracuda.

Maybe the only person who could have tamed the barracuda was my brother Bya. No sap he was, tongue sharper than a ginzu. We had several names for him: Madda Long Tongue, Miss Lashie, Lady B. And before you get carried away, he was and still is a boy—unquestioningly straight, if that matters. Bya understood he earned his monikers because he could cuss us clean out of our don't-wear-them-out-so-the-next-in-line-can-wear-them clothes. Like you never have a brother like that? Or worse, like cussing was a 'female thing.'

Anyway, he used to kimbo like Miss Puncie, hands at rest on di likkle mawga hips dem, mouth spread like butter in the sun and bwoy, he was ready for rapid fire: 'Seeya dutty gyal, nuh mek mi tell you bout you pawts yaw, try nuh badda wid mi cause when mi dun wid you, not even john crow nuh want yuh.' Just trust me, you don't want the translation; as I'd learned, some things are better left in the dark. Besides, he was good pedigree when he wasn't cussing. Good family fun. And funny enough Dee never really discouraged him, no matter how 'womanish' the cussing made him appear. She never encouraged him. But she never discouraged him either, like she did me from wanting to be an actress, often telling me "only prostitutes do dem things."

'Womanish' or not, Bya was my sidekick: the Trim to my Cykie, Cycolps to my Doslsemina, Starsky to my Hutch, cornmeal to my porridge, chamber to my bottom.

I helped with his chores; he helped with mine, except I always declined his invitation to help scrub the pots when it was his turn. Long before we were introduced to a dish washing machine or even knew there was such a thing, Bya was our resident dishwasher. It was his job to wash di plate dem morning, noon and night; we took turns scrubbing pots. We all fetched buckets of water from our 'neighbor with the pipe,' but it was Bya's job to use it to wash di plate dem.

If we played our cards right and waited till just as the sun was about to set before fetching the water, instead of washing up in a plastic basin under the tree, we got to shower in our neighbors' outdoor bathroom—under an actual shower. In other words, we wouldn't have to share the same tub of bath water, each washing up in order and degree of visible dirt. I'm not quite sure why we had to bathe before the sun kissed the sky goodnight, but we had to, and without question too.

As you can imagine though, timing was everything. If we tarried too long and the orange of the sky turned to brown, we would have to just wet a rag and wipe the pertinent parts, most important of which were the feet. We might have been permitted to go to bed hungry but never dirty. I guessed Dee didn't want us to have dirty feet in each other's faces as we slept head-to-toe to accommodate Bya, Stephanie, Mawma and myself in one queen bed. I swear to this day I can totally empathize with canned sardines.

But back to catching "water fi wash up di plate dem because yuh can't use the water from this morning to wash the plates from this evening." Only nasty people did that, nasty no good people. At least we didn't have to go too far to get water because that would have made it impossible for us to get back before Dee's spit dried. We got our water from Fat Verna, except of course when there was no water in any of the pipes in Seaforth, not even Fat Verna's as demanding as she was. Fat Verna could scare anything into submission but not even she could get Jamaica Public Works to ensure water in its pipes at all times. JPW was notorious for cutting water, with not so much as a warning. Fat Verna on the other hand, always announced her intentions, even those to kill or maim, half-murder or cripple. Before you judge us for getting water from a woman with murderous intents, just know that you didn't know her like we did. She was a woman of oh, a shade over five feet. Strapping, we called her. She was a wide as she was tall. Fat Verna roared always to make her voice box appear at the soles of her feet. Yes, we got our water from Fat Verna with the seven kids from seven fathers. (What, you didn't have nicknames for your neighbors?) Fat, stern, capable of murder Verna. I'm not just making up the capable of murder part either.

She was a braggart, in addition to all the darkness that surrounded her. She would often threaten to murder her eldest child Milly for not hanging the wash in the prescribed manner, or for not making the dumplings to Fat Verna's specifications: big and odious. Then one day, she came close to killing her only other daughter Sheryl, for stealing a slice of bread, not a loaf, a slice. As much food as Fat Verna bought she used it more for conspicuous show of her station in life than for the sustenance of her children.

Food was décor, fresh-fruit centerpieces, not meant to provide nourishment but to display status. I still can picture her waddling back from the market, kids in tow with baskets of display: fresh lettuce, tomatoes, carrots and beets. Symbols of good living, meant to be admired, revered, desired, but never eaten, at least not till after the fruit flies, and often the maggots had had their turn.

✝   ✝   ✝

And ye shall eat the flesh of your sons,
and the flesh of your daughters shall ye eat.

—Leviticus 26:29

Sheryl, like the rest of us kids, knew better than to touch whatever food her mother bought, unless of course it was going or had gone bad. More importantly though, she had had the good sense to not steal from an able-bodied neighbor who could have and would have chased her and beaten her before extraditing her to a worse fate at the hands of her mother. Instead, desperately hungry, Sheryl stole a piece of bread from Mister Mack, the only man in Seaforth suspected to be north of 90. We all thought he was senile, but learned the hard way that senility does not complain about hungry kids taking a piece of bread.

The absurdity was too much for Fat Verna. Having learned that one of *her* children had stolen food, of which she had an abundance of the best, like Mt. Etna, Fat Verna erupted. She grabbed Sheryl, fruit of her loins, and without thought of consequences, she held both her 10 year-old daughter's hands into the cast iron pot bubbling ever so violently in desperation to escape the heat of the wood fire on which it sat. Sheryl's hand sat among the flailing dumplings, yam and banana. Fat Verna was bellowing her usual gobbledygook. Sheryl was screeching her own version. Bellow and screech; screech and bellow. Before long neighbors had gathered, eager for get front-row to the spectacle. (It was our version of a Hollywood Premiere.)

Between the bellows we could decipher Fat Verna's admonitions: 'yuh naw go mek mi head look dung.'

Translation: You will not cause me to hang my head down.

Meaning: I'd rather kill you than have people think I can't feed my family. Her fat, an over abundance of it, was meant to tell all of Seaforth and surrounds that she could feed her family, that she was better than most. Sheryl, an unconscionable daughter who had had the audacity to steal a slice of bread was threatening Fat Verna's reputation for abundance. Sheryl had to be made an example to the other children.

Sheryl could easily have touched the sky: upon release she jumped higher than a puma. I was sure if she could have repeated that height, she might have been recruited to some school abroad where her talents for high jump or pole vault would be exploited. But who was to know it was the fury of the fire that had caused her to leap for the heavens. Hell, her hands had just met the wrath of an active volcano. And her release had come from my mother who had just threatened Fat Verna with a knife. How? Dee was less than half the size of the mother with murder on her mind. Anyway, Dee finally got Sheryl to stop jumping higher than the lines of clothes still swaying in the wind. My mother put a whole stick of butter on Sheryl's hands but that didn't quiet the shriek, that didn't cool the burn. Sheryl no longer had fingers; her skin and flesh were literally running. The melting skin formed a drip. My mother held Sheryl's hands under the tap hoping the water would remove the wrath of the boiling pot. Specks of flesh could hardly be distinguished from the brown earth.

✝ ✝ ✝

*In the sweat of thy face shalt thou eat bread, till
thou return unto the ground; for out of it wast thou
taken: for dust though art,
and unto dust shalt thou return.*

—Genesis 3:19

Dee, not Fat Verna, took Sheryl to Princess Margaret Hospital, oh an hour or so away when you could find transportation. My mother had realized no amount of butter or running water would stem the flow of melting flesh. Fat Verna, satisfied her daughter would never again steal a slice of bread, fed the rest of her children food cooked alongside Sheryl's hands. Fat Verna ate too, of her flesh, and she belched.

And thou shalt eat the fruit of thine own body,
The flesh of thy sons and of thy daughters.

—Deuteronomy 28:53

When we finally went to see Sheryl days later, I suspected we were happier for the excursion than the actual visit; a nice trip to an unpleasant place where death lurked. But at least the journey was itself an escape; we enjoyed the taxi ride past angry waves slapping rocks into submission, past views of the sky flirting with the sea. It was always nice to see waves gallop across the vastness of the Caribbean Sea. Sheryl eventually came out, ashamed of what *she'd* done. Her head hung low, her eyes fixed like those of a sow to slop. When her hands finally emerged from behind her back, they mostly looked like giant cotton swabs, not hands.

She didn't say how much it hurt, or even that it did. She didn't say how frustrating it was not being able to scratch an itch or button her dress or wipe her bottom. Sheryl didn't say anything. She didn't even repeat the ridiculous story her mother had concocted: 'Doctor, mi fall inna di pot and that's how mi burn mi hands dem.' I was disappointed the doctors thought a young girl had it in her to have fallen in a pot of boiling water with such precision as to cause injury to only her hands, starting at her fingers and ending at her wrists.

Like the adults had done so many times before, we just sat in quiet conversation, not exchanging a word, not even an eye contact. An hour or so later when it was time to leave, there was an unspoken, innate understanding, that unless we left at that moment, we would have missed *the* taxi that would bring us to the last bus going through Seaforth. Timing was everything. We theorized that if my mother hadn't rescued Sheryl the precise moment she had, the pain might have gone to Sheryl's heart and killed her.

Sheryl didn't say goodbye, she just put her giant cotton swaps in front of her, as if to keep our gaze from piercing her back, kept her head hung like a pig, and plodded back inside Princess Margaret.

After weeks of intense rehabilitation, Sheryl was released to her mother's care, back to the same house where she almost lost her hands because of a slice of bread. Everything was the same; nothing had changed, well, except for Sheryl's hands that is. The extra whispers and stares and murmurs were new. Sheryl's hands were webbed, showing no memory of fingers. Her web for hands made her look more like a duckling than a child. She could no longer hold a pencil, or button her dress, or hold a spoon, or play baseball with us, or steal a slice of bread.

We continued to go to Fat Verna for washing up water. It wasn't the only pipe in Seaforth, but it was the closest. So close in fact, echoes of Fat Verna bellowing for any of her children: Milly, Paul, Carl, Sheryl, Rowan, Sherman, Denny… "Come pass di plate gimme." Mind you, the plate was just outside her reach, and it would have taken her at least a couple steps had she managed to heave herself from the chair. She was a robust woman, quite possibly Botero's muse.

Her head sat directly on her shoulders, no neck needed. Mass Ken, her common-law husband whom she stole or inherited from Miss Shirley, was smart enough to spend his waking hours 'on the road.' He was a thin as the light of day and it made us all wonder how that stick of a man could 'control' such hippo of a woman. He was the original 'mouse pan a one-dollar bread' back when ten dollars could fill a scandal bag. You know, buy the week's groceries.

Anyway, that was where we went to get our water for hydration and for cleaning, from Fat Verna's pipe. Don't why ask but we weren't afraid she'd do to us what she had done to Sheryl. Even then we knew that she was hardly different from some wild animal that would eat her own, but would dare not touch someone else's. And like I said, her pipe gave us water no matter the time of day. Except of course, when there was no water to give, not even to women stuck with relaxed hair but burning heads. There were many occasions when women would scatter with heads on fire, if not literally then most certainly with burns to rival a two-alarm fire. They would have dipped their heads in a toilet, only that part of Jamaica still boasted the pit toilet, you know, an out house; great for accommodating waste, terrible for cooling heads. Screams could be heard all over town as women on fire searched for water, any water, to stop lye-laced relaxers eating their scalps. The only refuge was river; yes the same river with no name, just river.

✣ ✣ ✣

Am I my brother's keeper?

—Genesis 4:9

River was good. River was refuge. River was good, *clean* fun. We were always fully entertained jumping off tree limbs into some silent hole or walking upstream against water rushing to get the hell out of Seaforth. Not all the water was silent or in a boisterous rush. Some just glided. Have you ever watched water glide over moss-enveloped rocks? Peaceful. We spent hours watching water glide and snake; taking with it leaves and twigs. And we knew janga, you know shrimp, and suckies far preferred the quiet of the glide. That is, until we'd ripped them from their havens with our bare hands. The janga was far easier to capture, the suckies on the other hand, were more opposed to eviction. I was sure they had invisible suction cups on their bellies because they would stick to the rocks like, well suckies to a stone. We'd have to pull with determination to pluck them from their solace.

We preferred the gliding water, perhaps because we were discouraged from visiting the really silent part, the one they called Deep Hole. That was where Dee watched her "pretty" cousin Baboo drowned. When we dared ventured close to the Deep Hole, under Dee's watchful eyes of course, we were never allowed into the truly silent part so deep, so dark with secrets. We skirted the edges. Only fools or braggarts braved the dark. If the stories were to be believed, the silent water claimed lots of lives.

We actually watched Fitzie, so nicknamed because of his epileptic seizures, fight in vain to free himself from the curse of that part of the river. He suffered a seizure and had fallen into the river.

We had all gathered far enough not to be dragged in by Fitzie but close enough for personal account. We watched as he flailed and foamed, foamed and flailed. We were still watching as he just stopped trying and sank to where we couldn't see him anymore. Big bubbles turned into tiny bubbles and before long, Fitzie floated back to where we could see the current carrying his body down stream. It was safe to fetch him then—he posed no real danger. His brothers pulled his body across the stones and twigs and fallen branches.

I wondered if it was true that a person having a fit possessed the strength of a thousand men. I wondered why Fitzie's brothers waited for him to float downstream before helping him. I wondered if River was ever going to be the same.

✝ ✝ ✝

And he said, take now thy son, thine only son Isaac, whom thou lovest, and ... offer him there for a burnt offering.... and Abraham stretched forth his hand, and took the knife to slay his son.

—Genesis 22:2, 10

put on my panties, no shirt or skirt or slippers, just the panties and put the pan with the plates on top of the katta (a towel
or old shirt rolled into a circle meant to cushion) sitting on my
head. Bya, clad in only his brief, took the tub with the clothes
washed in the river, dried under the sun, folded to perfection,
on top of his katta. Dee fully clothed of course, she had things
to hide, put the tub of water on top of the katta on top of her
head, and we just went home.

We went past Fitzie's house where he'd had so many violent
fits. We went past the coconut tree to which Miss Joyce tethered her son, naked as the day he was born, and in the epicen-
ter of RIFA activity. Yes, RIFA, Red Imported Fire Ants listed
among the "100 World's Worst" invaders. Miss Joyce delivered
her son, bound and captive to ants with heads as big as coconuts
to feast on him. Was she hoping her son was acutely allergic to
RIFA stings? Was she certain he wouldn't suffer from nausea,
shock, chest pains or even coma? Even the farmers would move
their cows and donkeys and horses to shade but Miss Joyce left
Maurice, her troubled son tethered, without water, without
mercy.

Pustules made Maurice's body look like a human grater. His body was limp, defeated by the sun and though that wasn't the first time Miss Joyce had meted out severe punishment to tame her "bad" pickney, it wouldn't be the last either. The savage beatings did little to curb his appetite for delinquency. He was finally stopped, literally, when his mother hatched a murderous scheme, putting rhetoric to practice. After some other infraction, she had padded Maurice with paper, anointed him with kerosene, from the crown of his head to the soles of his feel, struck the match and watched him erupt. The flames raced from his head to his feet, and the more he ran, the angrier the flames grew. He had looked like a Hollywood stunt, only no one was yelling cut!

His body hissed as he finally entered the deep dark waters of river. The compassion of the silent water was stronger than flames deliberately set to a "bad" pickney. The Deep Hole was stronger than a mother's rage. The silent water had not victimized Maurice; it was merciful and delivered him, burnt but alive, to Princess Margaret Hospital. I wondered why Maurice was subsequently sent off to reform school for being set ablaze by his own mother.

I wondered why, like Fat Verna, Miss Joyce was never even questioned by the police. And the police didn't question Mr. Burger either when he slit the throat of his son, just like he'd slit the throats of so many goats. Like the scores of dead goats before him, Clinton's body just hung from the tree branch, as if on display, blood still dripping from the gash in his throat. I'd seen death before. I'd never seen my classmate hanging from a tree, like one of Mr. Burger's goats. I didn't know what Clinton had done to warrant his punishment, but Mr. Burger had been one of the few parents who actually said what they meant and worse, did what they said.

Death before dishonor!

✟ ✟ ✟

*If a man have a stubborn and rebellious son,
which will not obey the voice of his father, or the
voice of his mother, and that, when they have
chastened him, will not hearken unto them: Then
shall his father and his mother lay hold on him,
and bring him out unto the elders of his city, and
unto the gate of his place; And they shall say
unto the elders of his city, this our son is stubborn
and rebellious, he will not obey our voice; He is
a glutton, and a drunkard. And all the men of
his city shall stone him with stones, that he die: so
shalt thou put evil away from among you;
and all Israel shall hear, and fear.*

—Deuteronomy 21:18-21

don't know how I got so distracted. I was telling you about
Bya, my tall, skinny, good-looking bredda with the good,
no, great hair. He had teeth like the kids we'd see in movies:
straight, white and pretty. Bya, first child my mother had with
her husband Fin, was only a couple years younger than me so
we were close. He loved music; I tried to sing. He was always
going to be a musician, perhaps the reason he would beat the
hell out of the pots he was supposed to clean. When he wasn't
beating the hell out of the pots, he was inventing stuff. Nothing
in particular, just stuff. And when he wasn't beating or inventing, he was driving Fin to poetry: Bya come off a di wiya; Bya
stop playing wid di fiya; Bya put dung di tiya.

Bya did everything for me. He often risked the wrath of
the tamarind whip for me, his Dolsemina, his Trim, his Hutch.
Like the time he stole from Mrs. Hutchinson, the same yellow
teacher he inherited from me. I needed, no I wanted, money for
kisko pops because everyone in evening lessons had kisko pops.
I might have wanted kisko but I needed preparation for high
school entry exams, commonly known as Common Entrance
Exam. Bya wanted to make sure his big sister with 'di brain'

was prepared. He took money from Mrs. Hutchinson's purse so I could have kisko. Trouble was, even long after I passed the exams and started attending Morant Bay High School, Bya kept taking money from Mrs. Hutchinson's purse. He didn't listen to Fin's advice, "every day bucket a go a well, one day di bottom a go drop out." Bya's bottom dropped out. His face never lied and when he said, "Julie dem ketch mi," I'd already figured something was really, really wrong. At Dee's command, the tamarind whip whirred and hissed with unmistakable anger. Bya jumped, almost as high as Sheryl had done when her hands were being boiled alongside the evening's dinner. He peed and pleaded and promised never to do it again. The welts on his bottom and arms and back and legs told the story: though we were poor, we were proud and most definitely not thieves. Sheryl's webbed hands said the same thing.

✝ ✝ ✝

He that dwelleth in the secret place of the Most High
Shall abide in the shadow of the Almighty.

—Psalm 91:1

We lived in one of those sun-baked wooden houses where only tiny specks of the original blue paint remained in crevices even the sun couldn't penetrate. The verandah, a convenience for quiet conversations, disrupted the complete square. It housed a single chair, meant for only the most foreign visitor. Everyday folks sat comfortable on the familiar dirt floor, or just stand with arms folded across their chest, not because they were hiding something, but because they simply wanted to rest some part of the body. Folded arms were a sign of comfort, of ease.

There were three interchangeable rooms: one bedroom, a living room and a kitchen; or, two bedrooms and a kitchen, depending on whom we wanted to impress. Dee often changed *her* bedroom into a living room, which meant that we'd have to endure the concert of her muffled 'cries' and moans and squeaks of metal springs in her bed. We never understood why Dee never realized that the sheet she'd use to divide the room was not sound proof. We were not blinded by the night either. (Stars are so luminous when electric lights do not interfere.)

When the moon was good and ready, it sat in watch and inveigled us to do the same. We were glad when the cries would stop. It meant we could go to sleep knowing our mother really wasn't being hurt. We were doubly glad because our parents could again turn their attention to ensuring duppies wouldn't get to us. That was the one good thing about sharing a bedroom with our parents: they were the first line of defense against the evils of the night.

The living room, when it was a living room, was not for living. It was a showpiece, a showcase of status. A handmade settee, to be admired and not for sitting, carved from home-grown mahogany was the focal point. The red ochre-stained floors provided the perfect contrast against the dark of the mahogany. Lilies and ivies ran from the coffee table, down its Formica-covered legs unto the floor. The dining table, reserved for Sundays, Easter, Christmas and the occasional visitor, was made for four but we managed to seat six when necessary. A buffet, you know, china cabinet, protected the good plates and glasses; there was no room—or need for it to house everyday plastics. Hand-carved figurines, silk flowers, the current year's calendar, homemade curtains stretched across spring-like rods, more lilies in milk cans, and the bible accessorized. A dog-eared a picture of Jesus, deteriorating but revered, was nailed to the wall to the left of the lone window.

The kitchen was like a set on <u>Little House on the Prairie</u>. It was home to a makeshift oven. And I mean makeshift. Picture a converted oil container cut in half with a wire shelf (not sure how it was attached to the sides) suspended in the middle. Fire-red coal sat on the bottom, radiating enough heat to cook a whole chicken in record time. That makeshift oven baked many a potato pudding, cornmeal pudding and Christmas cake. It even served as toaster. To the left of the makeshift oven was a coal stove, ne'er two feet from the dirt floor, and that accommodated everyday cooking. Dee chose a coal stove as opposed to a wood-burning contraption. We could afford coal and beside, when we had to use wood, it was near impossible getting Dee's pots and pans to sparkle so she could see her reflection. Even though she'd coat the pots with layers of mud, the black soot still penetrated and stuck like suckie to a stone, conspiring to make our pot-scrubbing job even harder. Then there was the risk a wood fire posed: one pop or the wrong type of wood or too much kerosene would set the whole house ablaze. Ever see a wooden house burn?

A rickety wooden table, propped for stability, sat to the left of the coal stove. On the rickety table sat a largish white icebox, large pan for plates, one for cups and another for pots. Fin's water boots (galoshes), machete and donkey hampers lived under the rickety table. So did things with no names. Homegrown food including yam, banana, cocoa, pumpkin, dasheen, cabbage, carrots, and the like were kept in boxes *under* another rickety table. Store-bought food was put on display to say we can afford canned goods, imported granulated sugar, Ovaltine, Milo, Horlicks, good stuff. We were the only family on that side of the gully to own an icebox after all. Bya and I would ride Downey bus to the ice factory in Morant Bay— every Saturday. We'd buy a block of ice: 25, 50, 75 or 100 depending on which holiday was on the horizon. Getting back home with a block of ice was no easy task. Even Downey bus didn't want the dripping water; they didn't mind the higglers, hagglers and market women, but they didn't want dripping ice.

The few taxis that serviced points between Seaforth and Morant Bay were even more discriminating, especially since there was the issue of space. By the time they'd left the taxi stand in *centreville*, they were crammed to the gills, invariably with the youngest, prettiest girl straddling the gear stick. You've seen it? The girl sitting with the gear stick between her legs so the too-old-for-her male driver had to reach precariously between her legs to change gears? I often suspected the only reason a taxi stopped, only after my brother moved a few steps away, was to get me to sit with the gear stick between my legs.

By the time we'd get home, we would have lost at least a third or so of the ice; the balance Fin would chisel into chips then line the bottom of the icebox. Dee would stock it correctly; ensuring all the items that say 'we might be poor but we eat right' would sit proudly on top of the butter and other everyday items. Some of the ice would be reserved for Sunday's carrot or sour sop juice. And speaking of Sundays, they weren't just special because we had ice in our juice, ice was just a sidebar to the main event: brown stew Best Dressed chicken, Anchor Butter, Jell-O, rice & peas, shredded cabbage and carrots, string bean and then the ice-in-the-juice topper.

If Sundays were made for Best Dressed chicken, Saturdays were for beef soup; Fridays were for fried fish and bammy; Thursdays were for porridge (Ben Johnson day, whoever Ben Johnson was/is; Wednesdays were for stew peas; Tuesdays for rundung; Mondays for seasoned rice or anything curry: goat, saltfish, chicken.

Fridays were my favorite. I can still taste fresh fish bought off the back of Gullet's bike, gutted, scaled and escoveitched, or steamed with okra and Excelsior crackers. We couldn't have pork too often, it made Fin's belly rise to the heavens, falling back to earth only when zipper-closing sounds erupted from his bottom. But how I loved some good jerk pork.

Anyway, the kitchen was practical in its accidental design, sort of circular, lending itself to functionality and productivity. I supposed if we led an indoor life, we might have found it inadequate. But it got the job of meal preparation done efficiently. Everyday meal consumption was best under the shade of the guinep, mango or plum tree. The breeze would help cool the food for more enjoyable ingestion, and would at the same time, provide much needed personal ventilation.

There was no bathroom, but you already gleaned as much. There was a toilet just past the plum tree under which there were three or four graves. The zinc on the roof and all sides was a heat conductor, and often I imagined that hell would be more comfortable. The roaches and lizards didn't add to the ambience. It was more of a zinc tomb than a bathroom. And no there were no showers. The closest, like I said, was at Fat Verna's. Otherwise, we'd bathe under a tree with fresh rainwater, or water carried from Fat Verna's across the gully.

Our room, when it was just ours, had a queen bed that was to be made the second we our feet touched the floor in the mornings. It was not to be sat on, creased or otherwise disturbed until we'd washed our feet and readied for bed that evening. A make-shit wardrobe—a giant wooden horseshoe attached to the ceiling and from which a sheet dangled—hid our Sunday clothes from dust and nosy neighbors. Plastic bins housed our everyday clothes: from the clothesline, folded immediately to maintain the dried-in-the-sun freshness and stowed under the bed to ensure neatness. The kerosene lamp with the shade washed to remove soot and wick trimmed for maximum effectiveness sat on the windowsill, perfectly positioned to let approaching neighbors know when visiting hours were over. Additional pieces from the living room, when it was reclaimed as our parents' bedroom, ate up any space we might have had when the entire family shared a bedroom. Having no room to frolic, we'd file into bed: Bya in the far corner against the wall, head down; Mawma, head up; Stephanie, head down and me, head up. The logistics worked, two older ones on the outside keep the two younger ones on the inside, harder for them to roll out of bed.

Well, the logistics mostly worked. Stephanie had a 'weak bladder' because she was delicate. She'd even have to wear a marina, you know, an undershirt, on account of her susceptibility to catching cold. Anyway, because of her weak bladder, she would often crawl over me to get to the chimmey, you know, piss pot, near the foot of the bed. We dared not enter the dark of outside to use the toilet at nights. At least not after being chased by duppies Dee had to rebuke in the name of Jesus. We learned our lessons. Have you ever had to run from duppies when your legs were as heavy as a cement block? You'd pee in the chimmey too.

⟿

We had just finished our dinner of stew peas when Mrs. Hutchinson presented herself at our house—again. 'But a weh she a do ya at this time?' Teachers never went to parents. Parents were always summoned to teachers. Bya's face betrayed him and told me immediately he had been at it again; he'd been once again caught with his hand in Mrs. Hutchinson's purse. I wasn't sure why, I'd long been free of the dependence on kisko.

"Julie, dem ketch mi."

Bya's gaze crashed to the ground and by the time I found his eyes again, Mrs. Hutchinson had vanished across the gully. She had delivered her news and had sentenced my brother to another round with Dee. The yellow teacher was barely out of sight when Dee grabbed Bya by the right hand. Pee flowed freely, even before the first blow.

"A dead 'im dead now. A kill a gweh kill yuh een ya dis evening. Yuh mean di bwoy ca'an satisfy wid di likkle mi affi gi im. Julie go pick one whip carry come gimme." I would have been picking my own whip if I didn't pick Bya's. I tried to delay his 'murderation' as much as I could without signing my own death warrant. I had barely handed Dee the whip when my brother's supplication began. "Do Dee, do. Mi nah go dweet again. Do. Julie help mi, do. Miss Verna. Fin. Do Dee, do. Lawd jesas gad, do. Whoooi my yeye. Dee whoooi."

Translation: Please Dee, please. I won't do it again. Please. Julie help me. Miss Verna. Fin. Please Dee, please. Lord Jesus God. My eye, Dee please."

Meaning: Will someone, anyone keep this woman I've inherited as a mother from killing me.

No one was brave enough to interfere with my mother's rage. Not her husband. Not even Fat Verna, herself empathetic to a mother's shame brought on be a thieving child. And like clockwork, the dirt under Bya's feet turned to mud, encouraged by the pee still flowing even after his ordeal had stopped. Fresh urine mixed with dirt almost always turned to mud, especially when stirred by feet desperate to get away. Bya never stole from Mrs. Hutchinson again. He retired his sticky fingers for good.

⁓

My mother, the fourth of 12 children was born Diana Montgomery. The girl not important enough and with no room for a middle name grew up thinking she was born on October 7, 1943. Some 40 years later she would learn she was born November 4, 1943. Her siblings included sisters Winsome, Una and Deloris; good brothers Buzz, Junior, David and Verdel and rotten and predatory brothers Roxley, Norburt, Stephen and George.

She was a typical Jamaican mother, if you can typify a Jamaican mother of that time and place: She yelled, not instructed. She punished, not disciplined. She bullied, not modeled. She overpowered, not empowered. She discouraged, not encouraged. All her surviving children suffered some. Equal opportunity. Sometimes I felt I was her favorite I must confess. She was extra rigid with me; I'd put it down to higher expectations. With higher expectation came less tolerance.

By the time I came along on September 17, 1968, she had already had three sons. But at least I was the first girl, only one reason I fancied myself her favorite. If she were to be believed, my 'real' father Mumfort was the love of her life; the one who got away. And got away he did: before I was born he had immigrated to New York to be with *his* love, his wife, to whom his is still married. So, Bundy, my third brother's father inherited me, at least for the first 16 years of my life.

Most of my mother's childhood remained shrouded in secret. She offered only fleeting glimpses of some of the abuse she suffered, often making light or not even recognizing the horrific nature of some of what she recollected. Like her being beaten with a mortar stick, a solid wooden club used to pound coffee beans into, well, coffee—and cocoa beans into the world's best hot chocolate. The mortar stick, a supremely heavy solid club not unlike a baseball bat and carved out of the most enduring of wood, was apparently also good for pounding unruly children into submission.

Or her having to take the family dog on a trip from which he'd never return, having been suspended from a tree and pelted with rocks till *his* body acquiesced to *their* wishes—on instruction from her parents who did not want the dog returned home as he had consumed something he shouldn't have.

Or watching her mother camouflage a deadly razor blade in whatever food so that unwanted and unwelcome cats would take one lick then bleed to death.

Or her having to drop out of school in the fourth grade to become Pop's right hand around the house and in the fields.

Or that Mama, her own mother, had never particularly liked her, and that of the four daughters, she was the only one raised truly, wholly by Pops and Mama (Sophia, the eldest left for England while Dawn and Winsome went to live with Auntie, Pops' Kingstonian sister).

Or that Pops had rented her a room when, at age 19 she fell pregnant and unmarried. I often wondered why it was a worse sin to have a child out of wedlock than to kill a dog or cat in such a cruel manner.

In any event, as she would recall, she had her first-born in complete isolation, the only company the presence of the Lord who was there to witness my brother's passage into a world waiting to devour him. All was not lost. Pops raised Oin as his own child, and Diana was free to get pregnant again, giving birth a year after Oin was born. Nicholas, her second-born was handed over to his father Ray. Lanville, whose father I also inherited, was born 4 years later in 1967. He too, was raised by Pops as his own. I was the first of her children my mother raised on her own, at least for the first couple years before Fin, her husband came along.

She married Fin in 1970, and though I was already two years old, he told everyone he was my father. And he was. I claimed Fin, father to my three younger siblings: Bya, Stephanie and Mawma, as my own. I wasn't of his blood, yet he was and still is every bit my father, my dadda, my parent.

I wasn't of his body; he never tried to get into mine!

Dee would insist she was lucky to have met Fin. Who better to define one's own luck? After all, didn't she married him and as she'd put it, "settled down?"

✞   ✞   ✞

*Verily I say unto you, wheresoever this gospel shall
be preached in the whole world, [there] shall also
this, that this woman hath done,
be told for a memorial of her.*

—Matthew 26:13

As luck would have it, right after Dee married Fin, she found God. And having found God, she introduced him to her new husband and then to us and then to the whole world. And went on a crusade to introduce the world to Him; well she tried to introduce the rest of Seaforth to God, primarily through public prayer meetings held every so often in the district square. It was her duty to proselytize, to at least offer other wretches a chance at redemption. Everyone knew that unless the whole world accepts Him, there will be "weeping and wailing and gnashing of teeth; fire and brimstone will be the pillow upon which sinners sleep." I suspected the "weeping and wailing and gnashing" Dee passed on to her children—via the unrelenting tamarind whips, a taste of things to come, but with more permanence had we not accepted Him?

I always thought it ironic that Dee finding God caused her to morph into Pops: she already was a carbon copy of him, made in his likeness. Dee had long suspected Mama hated her for that, for being the daughter who looked like a carbon copy of her father Mama had married when she was only 15, and who plucked his new wife from the security of her own family in St. Ann to live in the back bush of St. Thomas.

In any event, Dee started acting like her father, a vessel of the Lord. She became an uncompromising servant of God and as such had to conduct her life in a manner pleasing Him. I was certain He would have disapproved of the way she'd beat us, often till we bled, but I supposed that was what repentance was all about.

Sin now; repent later.

And though the Lord probably absolved her of all sins when she used my own stiletto to puncture my skull, causing warm blood to snake down my back, I'm still working on forgetting the that episode and trying to remember what warranted it in the first place. He's also probably forgiven her when she threw a rock straight in the center of my back, yes along my spine. I'd imagined she was picturing David slaying Goliath. But she was my mother and I was certainly no Goliath, especially at age 14. When rock and back collided, some nerve or other gave out because I fell flat on my face, unable to move. That didn't scare her and though most mothers might have at least feigned concern, she mounted me and in her rage, shredded my beige corduroy dress with her bare rage-infused hands. Yes, I've been trying to but still cannot remember what might have inspired such rage in a mother. I do remember my brother Oin, then paralyzed by some unknown illness and barely able to call out in assistance. He watched, crippled, literally and figuratively. All he could do to help was cry. His tears flowed, as did mine.

"Yuh nah go hold mi head dung. A prefer kill yuh and beg God forgiveness."

Translation: You will not hold my head down. I'd rather kill you and beg God for forgiveness.

Meaning: I would rather submit to the pride of a parent killing a child than bear the shame brought on by a wayward teenage daughter.

Oin did the only thing he could, he cried. He tried to use his left hand to hoist his right hand to wipe a tear but by that stage of his unnamed illness he was simply too weak. And though he had lived with Pops and Mama when he was healthy and I suspected useful, my mother's ailing first born was *her* responsibility, her burden. He was brought to live with us in the new house with its concrete walls, indoor bathroom, proper kitchen, three dedicated bedrooms, verandah, living room, dining room and electricity.

And oh, yea, we had our own water, our very own pipes that carried water to the kitchen and bathroom. It was all thanks to the financial settlement Fin had received from his employer after the work van in which he and his fellow farm workers were traveling went careening into a canal in Florida. They had just finished their shift and were heading home before going out again on a shopping excursion. Fin had woken up in the hospital, unable to recall how he had gotten there, and worse, unable to move his left shoulder. He had to be told how the driver had swerved to avoid hitting another car but had failed to stabilize his own 15-passenger van. Fin couldn't understand why his body ached so much. He was shocked to learn of the almost foot-long cut on his shoulder, complete with a row of stitches meant to keep the newly installed bit of rebar in place. A part of Fin's scapula was replaced with steel. Nothing permanent from the accident, just a piece of iron, like the rebar used to make the house stand up to hurricanes, replacing his left shoulder blade. And yea, he was never invited back to work on any farm in America. That too was permanent.

✝ ✝ ✝

If a man say, I love God, and hateth his brother, he is a liar: for he that loveth not his brother whom he hath seen, how can he love God whom he hath not seen?

—1 John 4:20

was telling you about my brother Oin who was then living with us. More like waiting to die, his living was over. By then he was on year three of a mysterious but grave illness. The quietest, most agreeable of Dee's children would often cry out in agony when we had to shift him in his chair. He was always frail, but no one expected him to wither. Like Bya, he had 'American' teeth, straight white and pretty. His hair was pretty too; made extra wavy by the stocking cap he'd used to keep his hair down. You know, like grandfather like grandson. He often aped Pops' preaching too, and that made Pops very proud of the grandson who not only looked and acted like him, but also bore his last name. Oin Montgomery. Though Oin needed pillows to reach the steering wheel, Pops often let him take the car, unaccompanied. We never trusted his driving though, his head was barely visible above the steering wheel, and if you know the roads like we did, you wouldn't have trusted his driving either. There was the time we were walking to Pops' with Dee at the helm leading with a medley of gospel songs. Oin was driving toward us, heading to Dee's ironically and offered to turn around and drive us the rest of the way to Pops'. We met him back at Pops'.

Oin loved working on cars perhaps more than he loved driving them. He went to apprentice with Deedo, the-wholly-dependable-when-he's-not-drunk mechanic. Oin was apparently a prodigy and could tell us more that we'd care to hear about carburetors and distributors and radiators. Then one day, when he was 19, he fell sick, just like that. No great lead up; he just came home one night and he was as sickly as a centenarian burdened by all of life's diseased woes. Like any good Jamaican mother, Dee made him a cup of fresh-from-the-yard-mint tea; meant to be ingested as hot as bubbling tar, to dislodge the gas. Hot mint tea was the cure all. Oin belched a few times, maybe even farted and said the pain in his chest wasn't so bad anymore.

His pleas for hot mint tea were becoming routine, frequent, even excessive. After a while, the tea had to work harder to dislodge the gas. It's quite possible we were quietly entertained by my brother's heart trying to break through his chest in a mad attempt to acquaint itself with the outside world. Hundreds of cups of mint tea later and Dee took her first-born to Princess Margaret Hospital. The Indian doctor gave Dee a bottle of thick white medicine and though he didn't tell her what it was for and how it was supposed to keep his heart in his chest, she felt relieved.

The more the bottles of this medicine and that medicine piled up, the more violently his heart tried to escape the bony rib case it called home. Before long, his legs got really lazy, weak and stopped listening to his brain. They just wouldn't and didn't move when he told them to; they started lagging, dragging. It soon became clear the Indian doctor or any other at Princess Margaret Hospital could do nothing to help my brother's heart or to make his legs obedient again. I was then 15 and old enough to know my brother was grave.

We were soon on the bus to National Chest Clinic in Kingston. They had doctors from all over the world: England, America, China. Surely they, with all their expertise would be able to keep his heart in his chest and would force his legs into compliance. But like the medicines the Indian doctor at Princess Margaret had prescribed, the pills Oin got from NCC were useless. In fact, his legs got lazier and before long we had to pick them up for him. They didn't even lag anymore; they might as well have belonged to an embryo. Even a newborn can kick or fidget, you know, respond even if completely involuntarily. Before long, his hands decided to betray him as well; they too joined the boycott and stopped working. We went back to NCC; they prescribed more pills. They poked, they scratched their heads, they conjectured. They used far too many needles to create far too many holes at the base of Oin's spine. The holes yielded no clues as to what was ailing my brother, nor did the x-rays or educated guesses. I have since wondered if Oin, a boy who had barely ventured out of Seaforth, could have been afflicted with AIDS, relatively new and even in the most advanced countries was feared like the plague. We had never even heard of it in Seaforth, just as we knew coke to be something you drink. In any event, the doctors kept poking to try and give name to the ills that so ravaged my brother's body. They needed increasing amounts of spinal fluid to help chart his deterioration.

✛ ✛ ✛

Is any sick among you? Let him call for the elders of the church; and let them pray over him, Anointing him with oil in the name of the Lord. And the prayer of faith shall save the sick, and the Lord shall raise him up; and if he have committed sins, they shall be forgiven.

—James 5:15

We all took turns massaging Oin with olive oil prayed upon by men of God. He would be propped between Lanville and I, and with one foot placed on Lanville's left foot and the other foot on my right foot, we would take slow, careful deliberate steps, teaching his feet to do what we took for granted. It was a sort of dance repeated several times a day, a dance in which a father and his little girl might engage. But Oin couldn't engage, his legs only wobbled and buckled. His hands became flat; I'm not sure how to describe them other than flat, deflated. I had almost understood why Pops had said we were best equipped to take care of Oin because he was crippled. That was after he had prayed to God, pleading and promising and begging his Boss to save his grandson. God listened to neither Pops nor any other congregants. Not those from churches near. Not those from churches far. The fastings were all in vain. God turned his back on my brother; He joined the conspiracy and just like that Oin was on the recall list:

Feet.

Hands.

Skin.

Flesh.

Voice.

Saliva.

We replaced the mechanics of his body and even had to ease his penis into the homemade bedpan, a bottle, so he could relieve himself without bothering us. We had to sponge bathe him and shift him frequently to stave off bedsores. We had to put him on the toilet then wipe his bottom. We had to feed him. We had to brush his teeth. We had to comb his hair. We had to fan the flies from his face. We had to pick up the pieces of his flesh left behind when we moved him from bed to chair in the mornings, and from chair to bed in the evenings. We had to hope he hadn't noticed his missing chunks of flesh. We had to watch pieces of my brother float down the river as we put his clothes for the water to cleanse them. We had to scratch his itch. We had to put petroleum jelly on his tongue and in his mouth that had long been devoid of saliva, abandoned by fluids. We had to sit in quiet company, being sure to always be with him so as to keep the enormity of his situation from rising too much to his conscious. We tried to joke; to recall silly things, like Oin trying to drive us in Pops' car or him cupping his farts in his hands so he could hold it to our noses, of course without warning. We tried to look ahead to when he was better, and tried to be the first to guess, or come closest to what he'd want to do first when his feet returned. It was all nonsense of course, idle talk to keep from crying, to delay dying.

✠   ✠   ✠

And when they shall unto you, seek unto them that have familiar spirits, and unto wizards that peep, and that mutter: should not a people seek unto their God? For the living to the dead?

—Isaiah 8:19

After three years of fighting, we finally accepted God's will: He simply wasn't interested in helping the child and grandchild of his most ardent servants. And since God wasn't willing to help, Satan must be, if for no other reason than to flex his might. We, my brother Lanville and I, carried Oin to Bushy, the notorious professor shadow in Buff Bay in the neighboring parish of Portland. Bushy apparently could disappear and reappear at will. More important though, he was said to cure people just as he could make them ill, or worse, kill them. But we weren't there to maim or kill anyone, only to help our brother God was apparently too busy or too uncaring to help. If He wasn't going to help, at a minimum He should not judge us for finding someone who would help. Bushy boiled leaves and repeated verses and lit candles and rubbed Oin with oils—oils of all sorts of colors and smells. Some made us gag.

Gagging, or even going through with the threat, was a small price to pay to have our Oin live. And so, Lanville and I took Oin to see Bushy again. Then Roxley (my mother's brother) and Lanville took him. Then Lanville and I went without Oin when his body could no longer endure the two-hour dodge-the-potholes-ride. Each time the bus fell into another hole, Oin would wince an uncomplaining wince. It was just to keep him from dying, really. But we were not about to relinquish our brother ashes to ashes, dust to dust. Lanville and I never complained, not even when we had to miss days of school.

With pride and purpose, we dutifully endured the bumpity-bump of Downey bus, then that of some other bus so we could retrieve the concoction that *was* going to make Oin whole again. Overnight trips became more frequent as Bushy invariably had to harvest some bush at precisely the 'right time.' Too soon it won't work, too late, well, it won't work. It was during one of those overnight trips that Bushy made dinner laced with cloves—peculiar taste, a bit pungent. Maybe that was why Dee opted never to use them.

After dinner he gave Lanville a drink that made my brother fall asleep even before he could see the bottom of the white enamel mug with all its chips. Bushy held my right hand, much like George had done so many years earlier, and led me to the new concrete house he was having made. It had no roof and no floors, just steel rods sticking out of concrete blocks. The steel rods turned into fangs and I knew he would pick up where my uncle had left off.

How was I, there to save my brother, going to resist or kick or scream for Lanville? Why would I do something, anything to jeopardize my brother's chance at recovery? He took off my panties and told me I had nothing to worry about yet I knew I had everything to worry about: he was lying, even if he was the all-powerful disappearing and reappearing Professor Shadow.

Satan's servant, with all his might, lowered himself onto me and transferred the taste of cigarette from his mouth to mine. The slime from the mouth of this little dirty obeah man dribbled down my face and crept into my ear. I was entirely paralyzed, just like my brother I was there to help, except I knew my paralysis was temporary, or so I thought.

Bushy grunted as he went in and out of my vagina. He let out a grunt-turned-whimper as he pulled himself out for the last time. I didn't tell anyone, not because I was threatened or quieted by $2. I simply reminded myself that a *no every ting good fi eat good fi talk*. Besides, I was resigned to trading the remnants of my soul, and even parts of my body for the rejuvenation of brother's.

Bushy walked us to the bus stop and for the first time, waited with us until the bus came and we boarded. I never quite understood why we had to go through Kingston to get to Portland when Portland was right next to St. Thomas.

I never understood why people purporting to help only hurt. But at least we got Oin's medicine. I begged God, Buddha, Allah, Jehovah, Satan, whomever was listening to let this batch of medicine work. And if that batch of concoction didn't work, I asked God to take my brother so I would never have to have slime in my ear, the taste of cigarette in my mouth or grunts in my head.

Then I asked Him to forgive me for asking that my brother's life be traded for my freedom. But God wasn't listening. Weeks morphed into months and with each passing, chunks of my brother would be left on the side of his bed when we moved

him from bed to chair; and chunks would be left on his chair
when we moved him to his side of the bed he and I shared. He
whimpered like a wounded dog and *he* begged God to take his
life.

✝   ✝   ✝

*And she went, and sat her down over against him
a good way off, as it were a bowshot:
For she said, Let me not see the death of the child.
And she sat over against him, and lift up her voice,
and wept. and God heard the voice of the lad; and
said unto her, that aileth thee, Hagar? fear not;
God hath heard the voice of the lad where he is...
And God opened her eyes, and she saw a well of
water; and she went, and
filled the bottle with water, and
gave the lad a drink.*

—Genesis 21:17, 19

We learned that despite desperation to talk, Oin would get hopelessly winded at the slightest attempt to articulate a thought. His whispers had become nearly inaudible. He'd struggle to say, "mi wah go a toilet or mi wah likkle water or turn mi over or mi tired." Empathy became our guide. We had to use our own needs as the only gauge to determine what Oin might need. Months passed and his voice was now reduced to the faintest whisper. We literally had to put our ears on his mouth to try and hear anything.

More weeks went by and more chunks of flesh, some of which looked like scallops, abandoned my brother's body. His ribs were fully exposed, giving us an unwanted view of the human anatomy and leaving us to wonder when we were going to see his organs, especially his heart so desperate to leave his chest. Dee began begging God to take her first born.

Then on November 6, 1983, Oin whispered, with unparalleled clarity, where and how he wanted to be buried. We cried and assured him his was idle talk. He comforted us and told us not to be sad because he will be better; he will be without pain for the first time in three years; he'll have his body back—whole and for all eternity.

At approximately 7:30am, November 8, 1983, Dee came into the room as I was readying for school. She put her fingers under Oin's nose, as had become her routine.

"Beg yuh some water," he whispered.

"Too early man, mek mi mek you a cup of tea," Dee told him.

She returned with the tea, but Oin was dead. She'd tried to prop his head to drinking position but she let out a wail that went straight to Heaven, as though it was some code for telling God, 'he's finally yours again.'

She put her hand under his nose, her head on his chest, her hands on his belly.

She didn't get the response she wanted.

She wailed again.

Her belly looked like something inside her was trying to come out, to break free.

"Julie, come hold him head, try fi keep him mouth open."

She ran back to the kitchen and this time came back with a cup of water.

She asked me to hold his mouth open as she tried to pour water in but it was rejected, like our pleas to God, Satan, the obeah man.

The water just flowed down his neck.

She wailed.

She clasped her hands on the top of her head and wailed some more.

I swore *her* heart was trying to escape *her* chest. She wailed and gripped her belly.

She tried pouring more water down his throat. More water ran down his neck. His eyes were closed. His lips almost pink and he looked peaceful, finally free from pain. My brother was dead. I finished getting dressed and went to school. What else do you do until your principal tells you to go home and be with your family in the "great time of sorrow?"

Three days later, on Friday, November 11, 1983, Oin was lying in a coffin, the guest of honor. He had arrived early and waited patiently for everyone else to get there. My brother who hated to be the center of attention, who shied from anything resembling a spotlight, was on display for all to see and wonder amongst themselves if indeed he looked like himself. He wore a black suit—a three-piece suit—for the first time in his ever so fleeting 21 years. He wore no shoes; only thick socks to keep his feet warm. His hair was wavier than we remembered. His nose, already small, was frozen to a pinch. He didn't wince, he laid there quiet and uncomplaining as only he could. And when I eulogized him, I was sure he smiled.

My uncle Norburt, the only foreign guest, was at my eldest brother's funeral. Norburt was the respected, dependable son/brother/uncle. He had brought Oin his three-piece suit for his final display. He bought the coffin and paid for the funeral expenses including the radio announcements to let all of Jamaica know Pops' grandson was dead.

Norburt said he was impressed with my composure and with my ability to write the eulogy in about 10 minutes. I knew I was to read the eulogy, no one told me I had to write it. I guess you could say I wasn't versed in the ways of literal, physical death. I had known death, like that of my innocence. But I was unaccustomed to the protocol of physical death.

Anyway, Norburt said I should leave Jamaica, especially since I was graduating from high school soon. He said America had more opportunities for someone like me. Dee agreed without debate and seeing as though *Godot* never showed up in Seaforth anyhow, she thought it a good idea to send me to live with my uncle Norburt in Brooklyn, New York.

✝ ✝ ✝

*Blessed are they that mourn, for
they shall be comforted.*

—Matthew 5:4

Other than the death of my brother, high school was mostly uneventful. The usual was normal, expected. Disappointment was rare in the absence of expectations. Mr. Jackson, the assistant principal and track coach barked at us from across the field. Mrs. Parkins, the French teacher and wife of Principal Parkins tried her best to teach us how to be 'ladies.' The biggest standout, however, was not a bark or a lesson in etiquette. Since my first day at Morant Bay High School in September 1980, I'd been obsessed with our PE Teacher. Don't get me wrong, not that kind of obsessed. I was obsessed with his name, who the hell name their son Blandell? I was obsessed with the size of his afro. It was the dawn of the 1980s but someone had forgotten to tell him other people were starting to trim back their fros. I was most obsessed with his nose; I swore it was the biggest I'd ever seen sit on a face. Looking at him was like staring down the wrong end of a double barrel shot gun, sort of like a mosquito clad in the biggest Jackie-O sunglasses. They were massive and I was obsessed—he'd be the only survivor were we all to be stuck in an elevator. (Not that we had an elevator; I was just obsessed.)

Yes, Blandell's nostrils were among the few standouts. Other notables included the death of my brother, obviously. And oh yea, the loss of my two front teeth was a standout. I was well beyond the age when children changed teeth. I lost my permanent teeth, not quite as white or as perfects as my brothers' to my uncle George who wanted to prove his might. He had deliberately and great with malice, dislodged my teeth on another of his attempts to stick his penis in my vagina. He had been fooled by the lull caused by the grief of my losing a brother; he had mistaken that lull as invitation to once again try to hike my skirt and yank my panties. My uncle had thought my guards were down but I was bigger, stronger, more deter-mined NOT to be fucked with. And I was a bit of a runner by then, thanks to Mr. Jackson's bellows: "lift yuh back foot; swing yuh arms." I could run fast enough to at least delay the attacks that had become normal, expected.

If I was scared and confused the first time George tried to rape me, I was shocked and dismayed on the third and fourth and fifth and sixth and every time since.

By the time he had punched out my two front teeth, I was flat fed up. And I was desperately disappointed that my uncle's first attack had not been some fluke, some urge to satisfy teen-age curiosity, some temporary leave from sanity and things of the decent kind. There were countless other attempts, too many to list. But I had learned to run. And as I ran, I would yell, the most vile and inappropriate cussing.

He didn't like when I told him to "go suck out your woman." He didn't want to be told to "suck" his girlfriend but he saw nothing wrong with constantly trying to fuck his niece. George was incensed by *my* insults; he was hurt. And as fast as

I ran, he ran faster. I am still not sure when and how he got the rock he cradled in his fist, I wasn't in the habit of looking back to check the distance I'd put between an incestuous uncle and myself; looking back only added weight and awkwardness to feet in flight. Maybe that was the one time I should have looked back.

I felt his grip on my collar and had barely turned around when, with the might of pre-Delilah Samson, George punched me square in my mouth. Blood gushed and my two front teeth dangled, barely clinging to threads. I knew we had reached a turning point and knew even better to try and save my teeth. I used my tongue to push them into place. To my surprise, they stayed. The blood and tears and snot didn't force them back out. Can you imagine? It would have been impossible to be a teenager with no front teeth, no amount of wishing or singing, 'all I want for Christmas is my two front teeth,' would've eased that pain. And though we had lots of adults with teeth lost to age, neglect, decay, rum, lack of dental care, no care at all, it was wholly unusual to see a 'pretty' teenage girl sporting bare gums.

Not even blood-soaked clothes, two punched out front teeth, tears and snot, were enough to send George to jail. They weren't enough for Dee to go to the police or insist Pops did something about his son's insistence on raping me. The repeated attacks weren't enough for 'us' to stop talking to 'him.' They weren't enough for Dee to at least try and keep me from ever being alone with George again. That job would be left to me. Even so time passed, we all know it's the one thing that waits for no man. My front teeth, crooked and sunken in, were still with me. The reach of George's tentacles was still with me.

The stigma of George ramming his finger in my vagina was still with me. Bushy was still with me. Oin's death was still with me. All the shit was with me. My teeth though, would eventually turn black from nerve damage, but they stayed with me for as long as I needed them, until *I* had them removed for something more pleasing, something less inviting of stares and whispers, something that meant I no longer had to cover my mouth when I smiled.

That is, when I had something to smile about.

꩜

High school ended unceremoniously. I woke up one morning and it was all over. And like other decent Jamaican girls, I was shipped off to nursing school—without anyone consulting me, of course. But alas, I would have been a fool to object, it would mean spending most of my weekdays in New Kingston and away from George's tentacles. I didn't mind having to wake up before daybreak to make sure I got the minivan that left Seaforth at 5:30am, getting me to Morant Bay, the capital of my parish, by 6 am. I'd then hurry to get the minivan, the most attractive one that got me into Parade in downtown Kingston about 7:30.

Another half an hour on yet another minivan would get me to class by 8am. My socks and shoes would be free of the morning dew by the time we sat down to Anatomy & Physiology with Miss Hazel who tried to teach us country picknies about the human body. Of course we'd oblige with uproarious laughter at some of the foreign terms were we hearing. It might have been the embarrassment of talking about body parts, especially female body parts. Hmmm. Anyway, Miss Hazel had a Dickens of a time trying to control us when she tried to teach us about the female reproductive system: She drew a vagina the size of Kingston on the blackboard. Of course all of us 27 nurses in training laughed till tears flowed. We had never seen a pum-pum so big; we had heard rumors about them, but had never one the size of a prized pumpkin.

Imagine our surprise when she started labeling the parts using 'scientific' names: uterus, not womb; vulva, whatever that was; labia minora and majora (sounded more like Latin); and clitoris. Clitoris? 'Mawsa a wha name so?' Miss Hazel herself had finally stopped laughing when she slapped the cane on the blackboard, indicating it was time to get serious again.

"Stop the nonsense and get down to the business of learning." Yep, we had to get serious about learning about our own bodies. "You know the part that you call the pussy tongue?" Miss Hazel said with a straight face. "Well, that is known as the clitoris. Clitoris. Now everyone say it with me: C-L-I-T-O-R-I-S." We might have been able to get through the class if she hadn't told us to "own your vagina, own your clitoris, own your body."

"I want you all to go home and get a piece of looking glass and examine your vagina, look on all the parts, open it up and get familiar with all the parts, touch it, hold it, it's yours." It look like dis woman ya mad or something. "Get to know your C-L-I-T-O-R-I-S, not the pussy tongue? And it's not pum-pum or tun-tun or fishy or as dem boys call it, punawny. It is your vagina." I just remembered thinking a) where the hell was I going to get a piece of looking glass and b) where the hell was I going to examine my innards without being caught. If caught, no amount of explaining would have convinced my mother I wasn't being a "likkle dirty gyal." Was that something I really wanted to see? No thank you. I couldn't even get used to saying vagina let alone examine it up close and so personal.

There was only one person I knew who could say the word with an ease that made me suspicious, and she wasn't even a nurse to be. In fact, she was only the granddaughter of Meemie, the old lady wid di one eye. Meemie was all Paulette had, and Paulette was all Meemie had. Paulette's own mother had died during childbirth, and had taken the identity of Paulette's father to her so-so dirt grave. Personally, I couldn't imagine growing up with a one-eyed grandmother who cursed on the steps of Church, having barely made it before closing hymn. Then I'd get to thinking that at least Paulette didn't have uncles who preferred her to the throngs of available and consenting women with whom they shared no bloodlines. I made myself imagine that even with the one eye, had anything happened to Paulette, Meemie would be the first to see, and to do something about it. That was how much Meemie loved her Paulette.

✝   ✝   ✝

Be of the same mind one toward another.
Mind not high things,
but condescend to men of low estate.
Be not wise in your own conceits.

—Romans 12:16

Paulette wasn't like us in other ways. She was what people called a blackie tutu. She had big eyes and really thick lips too red for her complexion. Her hair could have scrubbed decades-old soot clean from charred pots. Paulette didn't care, or perhaps she didn't know she was a blackie tutu. Just as she could have cared less that I was supposed to be the 'hoytie-toytie stoosh gyal wid brain.' And though I was taught we all had our stations in life, I left my station to be with Paulette and she left hers to be with me.

We were friends. Great friends. We did friends things together: the good, the bad and the downright mischievous. Good things made us feel good; the bad things made us feel better. Like stealing Cheez Trix and suck-suck from piece-a-ear Gladys then yanking off her tam to expose the half ear she so desperately tried to keep under wraps. Then there was the time we snatched the dead dog from Mad Merlene's head. Sure, she called it a wig but it looked more like she was envious of some wayward dog's mane, starved it to death then threw it across her head. We didn't know the police would take Mad Merlene with the dead dog on her head seriously. *She* was mad.

But after Mad Merlene complained that we had hit her in the head with a rock and had yanked off her dead dog for a wig, the police sent Paulette to Famitary, you know, reform school for delinquents. No trial, no deliberations, just judgment.

I didn't see my friend for a year. I wondered why they never sent me. I quickly remembered I was Pops' granddaughter, and I was pedigree worth protecting. Well, when it really mattered; when not doing so would tarnish a family name. I didn't go to reform school though I wished I had had that luxury. I imagined it couldn't have been half as bad as the beating Dee doled; while poor Paulette's punishment was determined by the law, mine was meted out my by mother. Dee again tried to beat the unruly, wild tendencies out of me. I had barely got home when my mother flew out of the kitchen, fully engaged and speaking in tongues. She usually got that way when she sensed I was disgracing her honor or otherwise engaging in behavior that might tarnish the Montgomerys. I had heard her speak in tongues enough to know I had to muster every morsel of speed and run like Johnson River after a hurricane. I started the dash: lift leg to chest, stretch and strut. "And whatever you do, do NOT land on you heel," I heard Mr. Jackson roared. But this was no damn track meet. It was a dash for life—mine. To hell with form, I needed function. Engage the cheetah. Before I could get out of the box, Dee had pounced, turning the cheetah in me into a half-dead snail trying to swim in cold molasses. It was my accosting Mad Merlene that confirmed to my mother that I was getting too "hawd fi handle." Unmanageable. Rebellious.

A mad woman who wore dogs for hair gave Dee another opportunity to kick and punch and beat me. First with whatever was within reach: a chair, a shoe, a rock. Then with bare rage-fueled hands and feet. She didn't even cry, my mother never cried at the pool of blood and pee and defeat she'd created. There was no remorse. The fire in her eyes said enough. "If you ca'an hear you boun' fi feel. A nuh likkle talk me nuh talk to yuh, but yuh bruck stick put a yuh yiaze. Yuh nah go mek my head look dung. All mi know wah sweet nanny goat a go run har belly."

Translation: If you can't hear you will feel. Is not little talk I don't talk to you but you break stick and put it your ears. You will not make my head look down. All I know what sweet nanny goat will make her belly run.

Meaning: You *will* be beaten into submission.

And God knows Dee will use any excuse to beat even the slightest hint of independence or aspiration, let alone rebellion, out of the fruits of her loom. 'You will NOT cause shame to rain down on this family of devoted servants of God.' Besides, the very thing that attracts you will destroy you.

We took her seriously especially when she was fully engaged in her rage; when we could see our mother was not of herself but had submitted to a manifestation of a murderous villain. She often spewed fire, much like that her Boss has promised will destroy this world of heathens and "wolf in sheep's clothing."

✠   ✠   ✠

Beware of false prophets,
Which come to you in sheep's clothing,
But inwardly they are ravening wolves.

—Matthew 7:15

There were many wolves among God's sheep at the Seaforth branch of the Church of God of Prophecy, one of the 1600 churches that has earned Jamaica a world title: *Most Churches Per Square Mile*. Not bad for an island about 145 miles east to west, and 51 miles north to south. It might be something to brag about, unlike the other unenviable title as *Murder Capital of the World* (2005), according to BBC Caribbean. (I wonder where we rank when it comes to rum bars, most churches seem to be surrounded by two or three?)

In any event, I was telling you about our wolves in sheep's clothing, and in particular, Brother Jeremiah Truman, husband to Sister Primrose Truman and father to Lucille (aka Charm), Lisa, Glenroy (aka Guy) and Leonard. Time for confession: Brother Truman was not really wolf. No, he was more of a pig—literally; a pig of the cloth, a hog in church clothing. It was common knowledge that when his mother, Miss Puncie, was pregnant with him, she witnessed a pig being slaughtered. Not that pigs being slaughtered was outside the ordinary. Heck, I've helped slit the throats of pigs, goats, fowls, then helped cook them for dinner.

Apparently though, Miss Puncie was sentimental and didn't heed her own wisdom that as a "belly woman" she needed to steer clear of anything that could trigger emotion—or cravings.   Cravings must be satisfied. Failure to do so meant the unborn child would be born bearing evidence of cravings not satiated. If the stories were to be believed, she had felt sorry for the pig whose head she had seen leave its body. She had grabbed her face in empathy and perhaps thought nothing more of the incident until she gave birth to a healthy baby pig months later. Her son, Jeremiah, had been born owing the entire left side of his face to the pig with which Miss Puncie had empathized.

The right side of his face was human, smooth, normal, not particularly ugly or black but not handsome juxtapose a pig. The hog side looked like the skin of a burned animal, about ten layers thick. It was hairy, jet black and it looked coarse. It was so thick and wrinkly, in fact, it squeezed his eye shut and made the left nostril look twice the size of the right. The lips looked like he was in permanent Sambo makeup. You know, unnatural. Anyway, we all called him Hoggybus, which made his kids 'piglets.' Nicknames were part of the entertainment but to get the full value, the names had to be descriptive, like Slim or Bigga or Rum Head or Blacka, or Goatie for the boy caught copulating with a goat. Yes, nicknames had to paint the picture, rendering explanations unnecessary.

Hoggybus was our Church brother and more important, our friend. Like Fin, he traveled abroad for work: He went to Guantanamo Bay, Cuba (Gitmo) and Fin went to Belle Glades, Florida. Their annual trips abroad afforded us luxuries other families only imagined: new book bags and shoes at the start of *every* school term, not just when there was some scarce road-paving or dam-reinforcing work. The trips also meant we had materials that Dressmaker Geera would sew into new uniforms and new Church dresses. Fin, a tailor by trade would make all the trousers, Miss Geera made everything else, though she was nowhere near as reliable as our Fin. Miss Geera's unreliability had gone from bad to unacceptable in September 1985. It was my last year in high school, when she took my measurements, collected the materials and her fees but had failed to deliver my new uniform for the first day of school. She promised and promised and promised but when push came to shove, she absolutely refused to answer to her name when, at the appointed time, I went to her house to collect my brand spanking new uniform.

"Miss Geera," I called out.

"Miss Geera, it's me Julie."

"Miss Geera?" the summons had turned to questions.

When 'verbals' didn't work, I tried knocking. No answer. Needless to say I scooped up one handful of pebbles and peppered her zinc house with it. Yep, I made pebbles hail on the zinc roof of Miss Geera's house. Only when I thought if I didn't leave then and there I'd be late for school—in last-term uniform did I stop. After school that day, Dee asked why I stoned Geera's house. Well, I asked, "if she weren't home how would she have known I pelted her house?" I must have made sense to my mother because I wasn't beaten. Served Miss Geera right, I thought. (Renk and out of order, made me appear like we couldn't afford new uniforms.)

Anyway, as you've already gathered, I have a tendency to stray from the path; I was telling you about Hoggybus, the same Hoggybus who was Fin's brother in the Lord. But even as teeth and tongue will meet, even brothers in the Lord had bouts of disagreements. The brothers and sisters in Christ once had a quarrel that drew an impressive audience of nosy neighbors too bored with mundane chores not to stand in watch. The audience included the warring parties' children. We were more sensible though, and we made a pact with the piglets: we could still be friends even if the adults were behaving like temperamental lovers.

Dee and Hoggybus had been fussing about something or other, which meant, Fin and Hoggybus as well as Sister Truman and Dee were having a fuss about something or other. After minutes of verbal sparring, Hoggybus grabbed his wife, herself with enough facial hair, including the sideburns we imagined she had willed and cultivated just to convince the world she *was* her husband's soul mate.

"Come Lucky, come we go because if we never come a fowl roost, fowl couldn't shit pan we."

Translation: "Come Lucky, come let's go because if we didn't come to the fowl's nest, the fowl couldn't shit on us."

Meaning: If they hadn't stooped, they wouldn't have been subjected to such insults.

I never understood why they nicknamed Sister Primrose Truman, Lucky. What was lucky about having half a pig for a husband? What was lucky about having enough facial hair to make King Kong look clean shaved? In any event, despite the hog permanently residing on the left side of his face, Hoggybus still mostly behaved in a manner reserved for people with no flaws or at least with enough money to divert attention from their physical imperfections. Not Hoggybus who, despite his yearly pilgrimage to Gitmo, never really had enough money to stop renting the wooden box *they* called home long after we had vacated our own box for the concrete house.

Worse, he had to rent from poor one-eyed Meemie. It just didn't look good. And while most people would be grateful to their landlady, he looked down on Meemie—down the side of his nose unobstructed by the pig. He had once cursed her till tears flowed from her good, open eye. Maybe if he restricted the insults to Meemie, and not include her beloved mangy dog with no name, she would not have hurled the dirtiest words right back at him. Ah, siblings in the Lord slinging slurs.

Hoggybus had hit below the belt when he told *his* dog that he groveled too low and that he, the dog, had no ambition—for playing with Meemie's mangy dog with no name. Life according to Brother Truman meant even dogs, however mangy, were expected to comport themselves in a manner not to betray their station in life. You know, not grovel beneath them.

When Hoggybus was not too busy telling off mangy dogs or his church brothers and sisters, he was actually good fun, especially when he sang and played the guitar. And he was one of two townsfolk who fancied themselves professional photographer. Despite *his* unfortunate face people trusted him to make them look good on film.

It was nearing Christmas 1983, and Hoggybus had just returned from Gitmo, having missed the opportunity to immortalize Oin's on the day of his funeral though I think it was better that way. Oin hated having his pictures taken—he absolutely forbade it. All we had of Oin was his hand intruding in a photograph of us able-bodied siblings. It was obvious he could not move his had out of the frame. I actually ripped that pictures to shreds years after his death. It had been the source of too many uncontrollable sobbings; just a limp hand intruding. Like I said, he disliked photographs and I would prefer to have all of him, not just a limp hand that got in the way.

But there I go again, I was telling you about Hoggybus. He brought us gifts from foreign; gifts most appreciated since by then Fin was never invited back to Florida after his car accident. Remember the shuttle van in which Fin and his fellow farm workers were traveling, lost control and ended in one of Florida's famous canals. If the van was destroyed, Fin was damaged goods, not even fit for cane harvesting. Our yearly gifts from abroad were taken away, just like that. We had to rely on what little Hoggybus brought us: candy and books and pencils, never as nice as the ones he bestowed on his own children, but he at least thought about us, and me especially. He brought me special things. I was especially fond of the nice, lacy panties, not like the days-of-the-week ones Fin brought my sisters and I. Maybe I shouldn't be telling you this because I don't want you to judge me. Yes I know you are complete stranger, or are you? Nonetheless, I'd better try and think this over, try to get beyond the shame dripping from my fingertips onto the keyboard; the same shame that kept me buried for decades.

By now you should see where this is going.

Hoggybus had told Dee he was going to take photographs of me, for no reason. Just take photographs; to capture a moment; to freeze a frame. He had taken photographs before, including the only surviving childhood photo taken in 1977. There we were, in a straight line by age: Me, Bya, Stephanie, Mawma. Stephanie hated her long mouth and scratched her eyes off the picture as if to register her displeasure at having had her photograph taken against her will.

Hoggybus had his camera around his neck. Wasn't that how professional photographers identified themselves? He also had a largish bag with special equipment. He and I, photographer and subject, took a taxi from Seaforth to Morant Bay, and another from Morant Bay to Retreat. We could have gone to Lyssons' Beach but Retreat offered more options. Hoggybus wanted to go somewhere with fewer people even though I said I wouldn't have minded being photographed in front of an audience. We ended up at a secluded beach I didn't know existed, way past anything familiar. He lugged his bag of special equipment, camera dangling from his neck, me in tow, until he found the ideal spot, "best for scenery," he said.

Despite the words coming from the pig, my gut told me it was less about scenery and more about something sinister. We had gone past trees bent for natural shading, past boats tied to trees of an accommodating nature, past mounds of almonds waiting to be washed to sea. We had gone so far, the roar of waves crashing against the rocks had turned into mere whimpering. The leaves no longer whistled; they started sneering. I knew a sneer; I'd experienced it before with my uncle George.

Hoggybus stopped only when he was sure he had escaped all eyes, even God's I suspected. I didn't know exactly where I was, but knew enough to be very, very scared. Not a useful emotion as nothing good ever came from being scared. I would have been better off fed up, at least then I could have hurled insults and at best, end up with knocked out front teeth. He dropped the bag. I heard it fall, more than I saw it drop when he uncurled his fingers to release it. He took the camera from around his neck, up past the pig on his face and put it to rest on the ground with a palpable tenderness.

He told me to relax. He bent to unzip the bag. He told me to relax. He removed a blanket and waved it through the air until all the folds disappeared. He told me to relax. He let the blanket fall to the ground. He opened up the bag and removed 'foreign food' and placed them beside the blanket. He told me to relax. He told me to try the peanut butter sandwich. He told me to relax. He told me to have a piece of some sort of American apple. He told me to have a cup of the special drink. On any other day, I would have devoured the foreign delicacies. I was paralyzed to move hand to food to mouth though. He took his foreign clothes off to reveal the bulge in his brief. I wondered, though more to quiet the voices in my head, why he, the photographer, needed to disrobe; the subjects were usually the ones stripped to their bareness. He ate some of his American apple and grapes and peanut butter sandwich. He belched a hearty, self-satisfying belch. He washed the food down with his drink. He told me to relax.

The more he told me to relax, the more I recoiled, as though a turtle pulling its head in from unequivocal danger. (Isn't it funny how perceptive animals are of danger?) He took my hand and lowered me onto the blanket. He made sure my body was outstretched, as if a mortician attending the dead. He lowered the pig onto my face. Though I'd long imagined what that pig on his face actually felt like, that was not how I wanted to find out. He told me to relax. He pushed my skirt above my waist. He told me to relax. He pulled down my nice, lacy panties. He rubbed the pig against my face with such abrasion I was sure I was fully exfoliated, an idea I actually relished as that would be evidence enough of our church brother's transgression. Or at a minimum, would scrub away the sin of defilement. And in case you're wondering why I just accepted my fate, just know that no one would believe he, a man of God, wasn't tempted by some unsavory reincarnation of Eve.

The pig scraped my face as so many butchers had scraped the unusable from their kill.

He rammed his penis into me.

He told me to relax.

The pig scraped some more as it moved up and down.

He called out for the same God he had so many times on the pulpit of the Church of God of Prophecy. What the hell did God have to do with this pig ramming his penis into me? Why hadn't He, Supreme Being, stopped it? Wait, He didn't do much for me. I wondered if it was all prophesized. For a fleeting moment I wondered if Fin ever rammed himself into the daughters of his brother-in-Christ? A resounding HELL NO echoed like an angry thunderclap. I immediately felt ashamed and embarrassed I'd even allowed the thought to cross my mind. Fin was and still is a man beyond reproach, at least where that sort of thing is concerned.

I wondered how Hoggybus would ever look at Dee and Fin. It didn't matter because I knew straight away I would never again hold *his* gaze. I supposed he like so many at the Church of God of Prophecy really believed, wholeheartedly, that it was easier to ask forgiveness than it was to ask permission.

I wondered how quickly he would begin the vicious cycle of begging God for forgiveness, before moving on to the next daughter-in-Christ and begging forgiveness

✞ ✞ ✞

.

Thou shalt not kill.

—Exodus 20:13

Even at age 15, I knew that a missed period was never a good thing. Telling my mother was a worse sin. And don't ask how I knew, Dee never really explained even the simple logistics of reproduction. When I got my period at age 10, in all her sage she simply admonished as though I'd done something terrible, 'yuh can breed now.' That was the breadth of my lessons; not how to take care, not how to use and dispose of a pad, not how to ensure I didn't soil myself at school (which I did often), not how to avoid getting pregnant. Just, 'yuh can breed now.' I was afraid, very afraid of breeding. I'd seen the number of teenagers from less than upstanding families, who were breeding way too soon, and worse, who didn't know the fathers of their children in the making. I'd always imagined my own family to be carefully and painstakingly planned to ensure I rooted out all the seeds of incest and molestation. I didn't relish the thought of my children fucking each other's off springs. It had to stop somewhere, didn't it?

Anyway, I was telling you how I had missed my period at age 15. That in itself was not monumental. I was hardly 'regular.' Yet, somehow I knew something was different. So as not to be murdered by my mother, I opted for a proven tactic: write her a letter and send it, via courier Bya, explaining my predicament. The only difference was that the latest letter wouldn't contain something as trivial as a previous letter about chopping my hair when, without fruitless consultation, I had had my pretty hair cut into the latest rage, the Tony C aka the mullet: extremely short on top with a fish tail at the nape of the neck. The rest of my pretty hair was stuffed into a brown paper bag, with the letter explaining it was my hair and I could do as I please. That letter, you could say, was a test. It worked. Sending Dee my hair months before the pregnant letter somehow tamed her appetite for beating the disobedience out of me. It softened her. Or was she simply defeated and had given up on her ill-begotten child? Whatever it was, I had escaped with nothing more than a finger-pointing "gwaan, cut di hair weh God give yuh. When people tek you fi man, see weh you get." That was it? That was it. Dee was growing compassionate, becoming understanding.

I had hoped that the new understanding, at least what looked like the manifestation of understanding, would truly banish the beast that had occupied my mother. The 'pregnant' letter arrived, as expected, without delay. I waited till I knew Fin was home, had eaten and had all but forgotten the toils of the day before I left the library and went home. My mother was placid. Resigned. 'The calm before the storm,' I thought. But there was no storm brewing. No hurricane warnings. Just a mellow mother, who knew when to accept defeat, and who, despite her best efforts, knew she hadn't beaten rebellion out of me.

Or was it that she was unsure I was carrying my uncle's child and was resolute not to wear that badge of shame? Whatever the reason, within months of shedding my hair, my mother was scraping together every cent so I could evict whomever's bastard from my womb.

The bus ride from Seaforth to Kingston was always an adventure, an escape. I felt Dee's disappointment. I felt her admitting that despite best efforts her 15-year-old pickney was no different from the throngs of other 15-year-old girls. I even thought I saw glimpses of love, of care, transmitted mostly in softened glances from my mother, and perhaps most important, through her silence. Maybe she was being released from the glacier that had so long entombed her heart. It could have been her way of saying sorry for not protecting me. Whatever it was, I loved what it had done to her, and as we dodged potholes doing our best not to spill completely out of our seats, I wished the violence of the ride would cause a miscarriage, getting my mother off the hook for deliberately and against God's will, killing my unborn child.

In many ways I wished that trip never ended, maybe because I felt what it would be like to be loved by mother, maybe I didn't know quite what to expect in having a parasite extricated from my womb, maybe because I wasn't sure myself, whose seed I was harboring. It could have been Vincent's child and that would not have been altogether bad. Vincent, the Chinese transplant and proprietor of Seaforth's sole wholesale shop, was my first 'boyfriend.' Whatever that meant. I had given myself willingly, I think. It had first happened when I was 12. He was 34. I could have been coerced, I could have been tricked, I could have been curious what my uncle was so desperate to do to me. When Vincent had asked me if I "wanted to make love," in the back of his van, I had said yes. Problem was, I had no idea to what I was assenting. "Make love?" It sounded good, soft, inviting and so I said yes. Vincent and I 'made love' regularly in the back of his van. Sometimes the rice spilled and yet to be cleaned made it uncomfortable. Sometimes the smell of brine from mackerel or beef or pork reeked. But always it was good, soft, not forced.

The fetus could also have belonged to Doug, my high school 'boyfriend' my own age more or less, and whom I thought I loved but was never sure, mostly because he always did what I wanted, when I wanted. He once rewrote, by hand, an entire term's accumulation of my notes because I had lost my notebook. Doug was only two years my senior but somehow provided a kind of shelter and protection and decency I had not been used to, craved but unaccustomed. Whatever the reason though, I wanted more than shelter and protection and decency; I wanted things Doug didn't have to give.

The idea of not really knowing whose child I was carrying, made it just about impossible to picture what or whom it might look like. That was a blessing of sort. Not knowing made it difficult to attach, made it easy to evict without some pesky lingering guilt. But how was eviction to be done? I knew it had to be done, but how?

I soon found out that the doctor in New Kingston cared less about explaining processes than he did about the nameless, faceless, life he would soon suck out of my uterus, via my vagina. I said vagina, aren't you impressed? The doctor was a distinguished-looking man, not just because he was a doctor.

He was a totally white-haired man who looked about 60 but who had no wrinkles to betray his face. He might have been older, he might have been younger but whatever, maybe his age was of little consequence. However old, he might have been too bogged down by the scores of young girls peppering his waiting room. I wondered if he was one of those men who caused young girls to populate doctors' offices. I wondered if he was so cold, so detached because he just needed to remain neutral enough not to care, not to empathize. His glasses pinched his nose and I wondered why he just didn't take a few seconded to use his index finger and push them up. Such a simple solution for allowing more air in. Oh well, he didn't need air to remove the shame from my womb, just steady hands and a cold heart. That was not a job to the done with a normal heart, for that he would have needed to at least administer some sort of anesthesia.

⸺ϛ⸺

I'd never had to put my legs in stirrups before. Hell, I had barely been to *any* doctor before; we really never had the need. We had bushes for what ailed us: mint for gas, fever grass for, well, fever, aloe for scars, cerassie for bile, you get the picture. We only went to the doctor when it was necessary for admittance to High School. Yes, we had to be free from physical abnormalities. No once checked for emotional or mental maladies. They held firm to the adage: what eye nuh see, heart nuh leap. In other words, you only lament that which can be seen. As was mandatory, before starting the new term, we were given a form that had to be completed by Dr. Lighthouse, one of only three doctors in Morant Bay. The others were doctors Forte and Bonner. Anyway, before I go off on another tangent, let me finish telling you about Dr. Lighthouse. He was a formidable looking man with thick graying hair and white skin.

We weren't sure of his lineage, but it was clear he could trace it to places other than Africa. I thought he looked like he might be of Middle Eastern background, but what would I know. The only thing I knew for sure was that the doctor with the thick white mustache was more than a doctor. He was also a molester. I didn't see why he needed to grope my breast and finger my vagina, or why he needed to stick his tongue in my mouth, but that was what he did before simply signing off on the form. I had long suspected simply listening to my heart would have sufficed.

Anyway, there I go rambling again. I was just recollecting how I'd never had my legs in stirrups before, and not with my mother standing in prayerful watch. And most certainly not by a racially ambiguous man with pinched nostrils who just sat there shining a light up my crotch. That was just after he had instructed me to pee in a glass container. He had come back after a few minutes and said to my mother, "yes, she's pregnant, what do you want to do?"

"Well doc, we want to get rid of it," my mother said with a confidence I didn't know she had.

"Do you want to have it done today?"

"Yes, sar, we came all di way from St. Thomas."

"Hyacinth please come and assist, and bring a gown for me."

Hyacinth was the same mildly pleasant but mostly condescending and judgmental woman directing the front office. She was the same one who had told us to wait where everyone could see us. She brought in a faded green gown she threw my way. Hyacinth, who herself looked like she might have benefited from being evicted from her from her mother's womb, rolled a tray with all sorts of cold-looking stainless steel contraptions. She placed it close enough so the doctor hardly hard to stretch to reach. She stood in watch, passing one strange-named object then another at the doctor's instructions. Neither she nor the doctor showed mercy when I screamed or flinched. The sounds of suction made to mimic a slurp never left my ears. The business of a life being so violently dislodged, without the will or wherewithal to dodge the vacuum, can haunt a lifetime.

I never quite understood why even Dentist Tony, as temperamental as he was, never even attempted to fill a tooth without Novocain yet a doctor and his angel of no mercy found it entirely acceptable practice to kill a child, unborn albeit, without anesthetizing the mother. I was unsure the fetus had feelings, but I certainly did, and they caused me to conclude that the only reason the doctor and his angel of no mercy were so cold, so detached, so uncaring, was to send a message: 'however you ended up with us at your cervix, let this be a lesson to never come back.'

Indeed, perhaps the only thing more painful, was feeling every tug, every pull, hearing every instruction to Hyacinth, every throat cleared as the doctor lamented rather very matter-of-factly "why is this thing so stubborn?" I wished the pain would kill me along with the little bastard. But at least my mother was there, holding my hand and praying. Not condemning. Just holding my hand even when my throat betrayed me and refused to convey the screams meant to register the barbarism of what was being done to me, albeit for my own good.

If the bus ride to remove the unwelcome resident of my womb was torture, the ride back to Seaforth just hours later was death. Slow, deliberate, unhurried death, with not so much as a Panadol to numb the pain, you know, take the edge off. The doctor's voice ricocheted:

"Why is thing so stubborn?" Hmm, they'd always said I was a stubborn as a mule.

"My dear you'll need to have a D&C to make sure we got everything. You'll need to come back and see me."

Why the hell would I ever go back and see this mercenary of death who had called me dear only after he had tried to kill me? What I craved more than life itself was some hot chicken back soup or a cup of mint tea.

Years later when I learned that D&C meant *Dilation & Curettage*, I wished I had gone back to see him. But when I thought he was only feigning care so he could get more money out of us, I could have cared less about D&C, D&G or any other alphabet soup.

To my surprise, life went just went on.

✝ ✝ ✝

Recompense to no man evil for evil.
Provide things hones in the sight of all men.
If it is possible, as much as lieth in you,
live peaceably with all men.
Dearly beloved, avenge not yourselves,
but give place unto wrath:
for it is written, Vengeance is mine,
I will repay, saith the Lord.

—Romans 12: 17-21

I could have cared less about the stench of death that had suddenly enveloped Seaforth. I had narrowly escaped my own, or at least it felt that way when we aborted the life growing inside me. It had been a choice my mother made, and I was sure she had made her peace with God. I was less sure the young man from White Hall, a neighboring district, had time to make peace before he was sent to meet his maker. He was killed in the streets, in front of an audience unequipped and or unwilling to intervene. By the time we had reached what was left of him, the flow of truly red blood trickled from the gash that spanned his neck. I'd seen that kind of thing before when Mr. Burger slashed his son's throat so I knew his was a hopeless case. Apparently just before we had arrived on the scene, on the way home from night service at Church, the blood had really been gushing, not unlike when heavy rains caused the gullies to overflow into the main street with no name.

The boy's death was the biggest excitement and all the churchgoers and bar flies and heathens had gathered for the show, all eyes fixed on the life escaping a nameless teenage boy who should have been in church, not roaming the streets.

"If yuh live by the gun you shall die by the gun."

Only he wasn't killed with a gun; he was killed when someone or other had tried to separate his head from his body with a knife.

There was passive concern about who could have done it. The police were stationed not even a stone's throw away. And though the gathering of a crowd *that* size should have aroused their attention, they didn't arrive till long after a spectator, having seen enough of the macabre theatre, summoned them.

"Sir what do you mean someone has been killed?"

"Di bwoy have him throat cut sar."

"Where did this occur?"

"Right by Mr. Facey old gas station sar."

"You mean to tell me this happened almost next door?" the policeman asked with enough sarcasm to tell the drunk he was completely unbelievable in his assertion, to let the barfly know his was a tale of drunkenness.

"Yes sar, right where di gas pump used to be."

"Don't be silly, run along and stop drinking so much."

"But offica, di likkle bwoy, him dead sar."

"Show me what you talking about, and if I catch you drinking again I am going to arrest you. You understand me?"

"Yes sar, dere him is…"

"Let me through, people move back. Don't you people have anything better to do? …Kiss mi rass, let me go get back up."

"Wha yuh need back up fa, yuh nuh see di yout' dead?" asked one onlooker, speaking with enough volume to let the officer know even Ray Charles could have seen it was too late for the boy.

"Him nuh muss fraid a duppy," said another, prompting uproarious laughter meant to ridicule the officer and his attempt to, at a minimum, appear diligent in his duties.

The police cared little about the life of a low-level thug; they cared less about that boy's death and would rather not have had their heated domino game interrupted by some careless bwoy who had his throat cut. And to be interrupted by a known drunk was even more bothersome.

The unfortunate victim was an outsider, an unknown. We hadn't even gotten to know his name before his life was taken. As far as the police were concerned, he must have been up to no good. At least they wouldn't have to worry about his shenanigans. He was dead and some people were better dead than alive.

A couple officers threw him in the back of the lorry much like a butcher flung his kill in whatever truck, and took him to Princess Margaret Hospital, the only one in the entire parish. The rest of the police went back to dominoes. Though everyone knew who killed the no-name boy, no one said anything. It too passed.

In a way you could say death, and more to the point murder, was our primary entertainment for a while. Gunshots interrupted the quiet of night, their blasts muffling sounds from pulpits. Yes, gunshots rang louder than even amplified messages warning of death and destruction in the last days. One after another, men were being slaughtered and as they met their deaths, we all gathered for front row viewing. Nothing beat first-hand accounts. Reliable.

Some folks murmured, some shrugged. Others rejoiced. People rejoiced at the murder, especially that of John Space, a fellow resident with no real name, just a reputation for burglary and plundering. He was more a pest than a real danger; just the same, no one liked a pest. We preferred men who toiled and women who cooked and cleaned; at least on the surface.

When John Space turned up dead in his bed, still in his boxers, no shirt and with both hands cupping his penis, people rejoiced. We were even allowed to be late for school so we could go see him for ourselves. It was a bit underwhelming. There was not that much blood. No guts, nor gore. Just John Space cupping his dick.

I wondered if he had tried to fuck his niece or daughter or sister. If you asked me, he was fucking with someone he had no business fucking with and got what he deserved. It was kind of hard to feel sorry, really. Hell, if I had the balls, I would have shot a few fuckers in the nuts myself. It might have been a hobby of collecting the balls of men who touched who, what, when and where they ought not to have, and who didn't know sharing blood was all the reason not to share bed. I might have even killed those whose silence gave the predators approval and ammunition to continually hunt prey. Yes, I might have killed those who sat in silent complicity, who by default protected the guilty and leave the innocent to wear the armor of shame and abhorrence. I might have tried to kill the culture of complicity.

Anyway, days after John Space was found cupping his penis, Chinna was shot in the head. I liked Chinna; he was always nice. He was far from a pest. He kept a shop maybe as a front to something as we couldn't figure why anyone would want *him* dead, and so violently. Chinna was respectable, not like John Space. And more, Chinna gave people credit when they needed to eat and had no money, unlike most of the other shopkeepers who had signs telling everyone not to even consider asking for the take-now-pay-later plan. Not that most of the buyers could even read the signs that included "Trust in God, all others pay cash," "Cash and carry only." My favorite: "Sorry to inform you that Mr. Credit was killed. Funeral arrangements to be announced." Like most everyone in the district, I also went to Chinna's funeral. I watched his daughter wail. I saw the minister bless his body before returning it to the earth. Funny, Chinna had never stepped foot in a church, nor would he have on his own accord.

The things we make people do when they've lost the will to protest, when they are utterly and most definitely defenseless.

Even the police feigned an interest in Chinna's murder. It may very well have been because of his Chinese heritage. They started poking around, asking obligatory questions, like why, and who could have done this? The how was clear. He had been shot in the head and the heart. The bullet in his head had escaped through his left eye. I wondered why the eyeball just dangled and why it was strong enough to endure the blast of a bullet. I wondered if the mortician had pushed it back in before loading Chinna into the coffin.

We all wondered who'd be next and didn't have to wait long to find out that Dudley wore the mark of death. He needed to sleep on the same side though because something in him made him live despite being shot in the head, in front of his father. They say a dead man tells no tales. Well apparently neither do men who had returned from the dead. Dudley lived, but never told.

As you can imagine, the rumor mill was in overdrive and the most credible, most prolific theory was that Michael

Manley had done a better job than his political rival Edward Seaga arming soldiers for the upcoming elections. It might very well have been. After all, you couldn't even be caught wearing the wrong color during election time. You'd be marking yourself for death for wearing orange in a green zone. So you see why people would make such assumptions that political rivals hired rogues to wipe out competition. The killings seemed so very targeted. My sister Stephanie and I actually ran into one of, if not the lone killer, as we left Fin's father's house. It had seemed odd that in the unforgiving sun of Jamaica, he was wearing a trench coat. He was on a mission, with just enough time to tell us to go home and stay inside. That night Blue and Gawgo met their maker having had their heads and hearts shredded by bullets. Days later, the trench-coated stranger was himself shot in the head by the police. He died. The police paraded his unclad body through Seaforth, as if to say, there, if you live by the gun, you shall die by the gun. And just like that, the killings came to an end.

For a good month or so, we had nonstop entertainment, far more consistent and predictable than that offered by our sole television station, the Jamaica Broadcasting Corporation. The JBC was not only wildly unpredictable, we had to watch it, when it was on, in boring black & white.

We had come to prefer what the rest of the world had: full color. The fresh blood of murder victims was best viewed in vivid color. Not some simulated interpretation.

✝   ✝   ✝

Ye have heard how I said unto you, I go away,
and come [again] unto you.
If ye loved me, ye would rejoice, because I said so,
I go unto the Father:
For my Father is greater than I.

—John 14:28

It was the mid-1980s and Whitney Houston was at the top of the charts with *Saving All My Love For You*. And if she, a lanky black girl who reminded me of my own reflection, could sing about saving all her love, well, I would at least try not to give all of mine away; no matter the promises. I'd learned not to take too much refuge or put too much stock in promises; I'd seen too many melt like butter 'gainst sun. Even I had gotten to believe a promise is of comfort to a fool, and was dead set on never again relying on the solace of a promise. I'm still not sure why I fell for Mumfort Taylor's promises: "I will come back and get you." Actually, Mumfort had made that same promise years earlier, 1978 to be exact.

I had been waiting since 1978 for the fulfillment of Mumfort's promise, and had often pictured myself living with my father in New York. Yes, I said my father. Don't get me wrong, Fin was and still is the only father I'd really ever *known*, and remains the only one I ever loved. Period. But as long as I could remember Dee, for whatever reason, always made sure I knew my "real father" was Mumfort. In fact, it had become sort of a mantra, "A Mumfort Taylor a yuh puppa mawsa, a nuh Bundy."

Translation: "Mumfort Taylor is your father, not Bundy."

Meaning: While there is life there is hope that Mumfort would one day return to claim what was rightfully his, me. And I long suspected that, for my mother, it was some sort of package deal, she being an undeniable, if not primary part.

Unfortunately other than the weird encounter in 1978 when the strange man visited our house on the side of the gully, there had been no further contact. He was strange in so many ways: he wore sandals with black socks pulled up to just below the knees; he spoke funny, using complete English sentences; he wore glasses, expensive looking glasses. He didn't say much to me. After he'd finished talking in private to Dee, he came up to me, hoisted my dress above me head, twirled me to expose my panties so he could get a good look at my right side. For some reason I wasn't scared when he did that, he was a stranger, not an uncle. He let my dress fall before putting his hand under my chin to turn the left side of my face toward him. He felt my mole, just like he'd felt the mole on my over exposed side, and made his declaration: "yes, she is mine." I had passed inspection, one mole at a time. Mumfort's visit had ended with the promise, "I will come back for you." Wow, a stranger who had hoisted my dress with no sinister motive was coming to get me, to free me from my uncle hoisting my dress. Wow!

The days raced into weeks that slowed into months. The years passed and the promise faded. I went back to Bundy. Remember, though I'd never known a life without Fin, Dee always told me he wasn't my father. Fin was a convenient stand in, just as Bundy had been. But all that wishing and hoping was starting to be a burden, more trouble than it was worth, so I did what came naturally—I buried it all. I'd become expert at stowing things in the miles-deep crevices of my mind. Some have still remained hidden. Yes, I shelved Mumfort and his promise. I reclaimed Fin as my father. Bundy hardly matter. He had never acted like a father.

I might have buried Mumfort but the rest of Seaforth and surrounds apparently did not; they had more difficulty forgetting the strange mole inspector. How could they have known, you wonder? Well, Seaforth was one of those districts where everyone knew everyone, and worse, everyone knew everyone's business. Hell, even the trees had eyes and ears. Some had mouths too because though I hadn't said anything (how would I have started that conversation?), everyone was put on alert: Fin wasn't my father. Nor was Bundy, who had been assigned ownership since my birth. I might have told you this but at times I had to force myself to reconcile that before my younger siblings (Bya, Stephanie and Mawma), Lanville and I were the only ones to share the same last name, Mignott. Oin was a Montgomery. Nicholas was a Smith. Lanville and I were Mignotts. Obviously though, Bundy had only been blessed with temporary fatherhood of some bastard gyal, not that he did anything with his blessings, mind you. Actually Bundy did a lot. He bragged about him "bright daughter." And he too made lots of promises. "Come meet mi dung a Miss Icy bar fi some money fi school; come meet mi up a Serge pay day; come meet me over Miss Cherry bar fi some money fi books."

Lanville and I were often desperate or greedy enough to actually go in search of our 'father.' There weren't many places to look though, when he was in Seaforth he was at Miss Icy bar, Miss Cherry bar, Miss Joyce bar or any other rum bar. When we were lucky enough to find him, he always bought us a cola champagne or pineapple soda, often enough to quiet the desperation, to satisfy the greed. We sometimes tried to outsmart Bundy and tried to meet him at Serge Island Dairies where he worked, but somehow the week's pay would hasten his departure and chase him into the nearest rum bar.

Of all the rum bars though, Miss Icy's was his favorite. That's where we mostly found him, only rarely were we fortunate enough to get there before he was too pissed to recognize his bastard son and jacket daughter. (When a man is "given" a child that is clearly not his, folks would call that child a jacket.) Come to think of it, I don't remember him not being pissed; eyes opened only with absolute determination; head swaying from left to right; walk reduced to chaotic exaggerated steps; hands operating in slow motion as he summoned another round of overproof unadulterated white rum; speech slurred to a "shiddung ova de sho, yuh want a, ah, ahhh… shoda?" By all accounts, he'd earned his nickname, Pissa. I had a Pissa for a father. But at least through him I inherited a name with a ring to it: Julie Marie Mignott. Well, at least I had a name with a ring for the first 16 years of my existence. Daisy Rumford, nice ring too, recognized the name Mignott during our first day of Morant Bay High School back in September 1980.

"Julie Mignott?"

"Here Mr. Stephens." 'Bwoy what a nose God cuss you wid,' I thought, praying I had said what I was supposed to and not what I was thinking.

I wasn't expecting Roll Call; we were in high school. Anyway, Daisy recognized the name Mignott because apparently not too many folks in town had it, and if you were lucky enough to come by it, whatever the means, you were kin. I didn't recognize her name as common as Bauxite, but that didn't stop the excitement from spilling.

"You must be my cousin," she said in a perfect English sentence.

Sure enough her mother confirmed, and Dee, said oh yea, her mother, Tina and Bundy are first cousins. That made Daisy and I close kin. We shared the same great grandmother, Nana. Daisy became Daze, and I became her bosom buddy. I was glad to ease into high school with someone who had had experience being hoytie toytie. High school was after all a distinction, not some dibby-dibby secondary school. Only smart kids who had passed their Common Entrance exam could even dream about High School. I would learn a lot from Daze and before long, Sharon joined the click, taking us from chamber-and-bottom cousins to the I-Threes. Yea, that I-Threes, Bob Marley's backup singers: Rita Marley, Marcia Griffiths and Judy Mowatt. We weren't sure which of us was Rita, Marcia or Judy. It really didn't matter. We were inseparable: Daze and me, her newfound cousin. Sharon aka Floweca Bawcawa was the turd, I mean third. She had earned the nickname when some random guy walked into our classroom, pointed at her and said, "My name is Floweca Bawcawa, what's yours?" It didn't take much for a name to stick; we were bored. That's why they called me big nut I guessed; sounded like Mignott. Go figure.

In any event, Daze, Floweca and Big Nut made our teachers, especially Mr. Jackson, the original Wacko Jacko, wished they had chosen different career paths. You know, ones that didn't call for them trying to train ingrates. We loved our teachers, well most of them. We definitely loved Wacko Jacko. More than a track coach, he tried to teach us conformity, like wear the designated uniform, in the proper manner. I suspected we were like every other teenager, mostly. We went from first form to fifth form, from crushes to boyfriends, from virgin hair to relaxed mane, all while wearing one foot of the other's shoe, so at the end of it all, we'd all be wearing mismatched shoes. That was our trademark. And though the strict Methodist dress code called for tunics below the knees—in green, white blouses with sleeves to the elbow, white socks pulled up mid shin and black shine-like-diamond shoes, we opted for brown shoes, ankle socks, sleeves rolled to a triangle atop our shoulders and a tunic well above the knee—and with an absolutely forbidden belt worn underneath, to create the illusion of a waistline. Heck, sometimes we wore the absolutely forbidden belt on the outside. Rebellious. Radical.

Poor Wacko Jacko, damned near had a heart attack when the I-Threes showed up at school, in uniform, and each wearing her own *black* shoes. Mr. Jackson's usual gruff was replaced with a grin. He actually called us up on the dais during Assembly and pointed at our feet. Mr. Jackson, deputy headmaster and track coach feared by all, waved his hand at our feet. We sashayed across the stage, obligingly, and curtsied at the applause. That was probably the last time we were in sync. Don't get me wrong; Daze, Flower and I were truly inseparable. And while I loved my friend Flower, I adored my cousin courtesy of Bundy. Until she uncharacteristically crossed the line, that is. I was used to people crossing the line, but when Daze joined the chorus of relatives who betrayed, the hurt was unbearable. She was a Rumford, no kin, no connection to Montgomery.

What gave her the right to betray?

She had crossed the line. The same line she told Dee was too old for me, no good for me. She had started secretly seeing Fitzroy Scott, the same police constable she told my mother meant me no good. I had simply had enough of relatives behaving badly. I, having gotten to school extra early that particular Wednesday, not bothering to wait so Daze and I could take the same taxi. I used the blackboard (no it wasn't called a chalkboard in those days) to let the entire class know of Daze's betrayal. With ne'er the slightest attempt to camouflage my handwriting I wrote:

"Di gyal wid di biggest mout inna di class a man tief."

Yes, I should have known better as a fourth former. Just as she should have know better as a cousin not to stoop below the line, not to grovel lower than Hoggybus' dog when she started sleeping with *my* man. Naturally, she saw the note meant to humiliate. Everyone watched as we fought like two bulls fighting to stake claim to the same pen. The only thing missing was the foam at the mouth.

I won that fight fair and square. I was the attacker, more aggression to release, more of everything to prove. I had had way more experience fighting off fuckers. I had learned to take aggression out on women, not the men whom I might not be able to beat. Women were easy prey. I had even taken to walking around with cornmeal in my pocket. Cornmeal made fighting 'bigger' women a breeze. A handful of cornmeal in the eyes, immobilized many any female foe. The tiniest amount, I learned, was too much of an irritant to the eyes and most definitely kept the opponent blinded. I had even started fighting effeminate males, like Wesley, whom I had properly beaten. I had help though. My grandmother had apparently recognized my dress as I was fully engaged in a fight with Wesley. Rather than try to separate us, Mama held him so I could beat him without having to fend off his blow. The policeman who eventually showed up, beat Wesley again. His justification? 'Never fight a girl and never let a girl beat you.'

It wasn't the first time I fought Wesley, he was weak, easily beaten. Frankly, I was getting bored with Wesley. I had nearly ripped out his eye socket, and when his mother had come to complain to my mother, well, she left before she too could be beaten to a pulp.

And I had damn near ripped Miss Morgan's flesh from her arm, of course before I had had my front teeth knocked out by a pedophilic uncle. But if you ask me, as a teacher in training Miss Morgan should have known better than to attack me at school though. So what she was a teacher? *She* should have known better than to take a leather strap to me. I might have been plain tired of being preyed upon; I might have enjoyed being the victor. I had definitely enjoyed sinking my teeth into the fat of her arm, and even with two male teachers trying to pry me off, did not let go. Her blood did not deter me either. In that moment I had known what it meant to be a lion devouring fresh kill.

Then there was the time Kenroy and I got into a fight for whatever the reason. I had given him a rage-fueled beating

but was not altogether convinced it was a decisive TKO.
Never one to accept a draw, I went to my uncle Trevor for
'support.' Trevor and I waited for Kenroy, a passenger on the
crossbar of *his* uncle's bicycle. Naturally, Trevor told me to
pull Kenroy off the bicycle in motion. I had suspected Kenroy
might have alerted his uncle, because after I pulled him off
the moving bicycle, *his* uncle kept riding, perhaps not real-
izing he had lost his passenger cargo. Then again, it might
have been the fact the Trevor was known as the Goliath of
Seaforth.

I beat Kenroy till I was weak from fatigue. I was satisfied.
But, there I go again. I was telling you about Daze and I fighting
like two roosters staking claim to a henhouse. Mr. Supria, or as
we called him S-U-P-R-I-A, our biology teacher, watched with
arms folded across his chest, and when he was satisfied we had
cooled down and he was in no danger of getting caught in the
crossfire, he marched us to Mr. Parkins' office. It was never a
good thing to be brought to the principal's office. Never. I tried
to remain cool on the surface as the years of familial betrayal
bubbled beneath. I was about to blow like a pressure cooker pot
atop too much heat. Heck, I had every right to send a message
that I was not to be messed with, and Daze, a girl my size I
could take on; unlike my uncle or other grown men. Why the
hell not seize the opportunity to pounce, to accost; to be the
aggressor?

I was going to take a stand against blood betraying blood.
Even after Mr. Parkins had told us we were both suspended
for "behaving like hooligans" I went straight back to class that
day, and everyday of the supposed 10-day suspension. Nobody
told me to go home, nobody asked what I was doing in school

having been suspended. Nobody asked if I knew what suspension meant.

The "disciplinary action" never showed up on my 'record.' In other words, *it* didn't haunt me. Lots of things haunted me, but not that. The strained, if not broken relationship with Daze haunted me. My uncle's tentacles haunted me. Sheryl's hands haunted me. Clinton's neck haunted me. My brother's death haunted me. So I was glad to have been given a break. Look at me; I had started out telling you about Bundy, didn't I? But you'll have to forgive me, that kind of ranting tends to happen when I try to clear out the crevices in my head.

Back to Bundy, who like so many Jamaicans, had a name that everyone knew. Bundy. He also had a name you'll be surprised to learn is the real thing. Bundy's was Ulando. Ulando 'Bundy' Mignott. I guessed his generation didn't have time for middle names. He was just Ulando Mignott, grandson of Nana, son of Miss Mama. Brother to Alman, Zelda, Nena, Vill (some christened names, some nicknames, I don't know the difference). Bundy was a son-of-a-bitch, maybe not literally because I scarcely knew his mother. He was a drunk. He was also an illiterate and everybody knew that, just like they all knew he was a father in name not in deed. He was a deadbeat. I wasn't sure I wanted to feel sorry for him when Mumfort, 'my real father' returned to Jamaica in 1984, nearly a decade since he hoisted my dress, to relieve Bundy of the burdens of being father to me.

✝ ✝ ✝

"If a man vow a vow unto the Lord, or swear an oath to bind his soul with a bond; he shall not break his word, he shall do according to all that proceedeth out of his mouth."

—Numbers 30:2

Mumfort Taylor had finally returned to fulfill his promise. He brought me clothes and my own peanut butter and cookies and books and what not. He didn't know my size, nor had he bothered to ask so the clothes were too big, way too big, meant for someone three times my size. But at least he brought me clothes from abroad, and that was a band-aid on the wound he had inflicted with his 1978 empty promise. I was less sore when he *had* returned to reclaim what which was his, me. He had pulled up in his fancy rental car, his socks and sandals and his cheap-ass clothes, highlighted by his dwarf-the-face glasses and his too-black-fi-deh-a-foreign skin.

Mumfort had again announced with words that ricocheted, much like that scene in *Star Wars*, 'I AM YOUR FATHER!' That was just after he'd again hoisted my dress and checked my mole, I guessed to ensure they were still there and not some trickery nearly a decade earlier. They were still there, in the same place: one on the far end of my left cheek and another halfway between my armpit and waist on my right side. Phew!

Unlike his guest appearance in 1978, Mumfort's 1984 visit had a sense of urgency, dire straits. Whatever he had planned couldn't have waited another six years, six months or six seconds; absolutely no tarrying. I guessed he forgot time was indeed longer than rope, and that there was no need to act with such haste. Everybody but him knew haste almost always resulted in waste. Dee and I climbed into his rental with the 'RR' in the license plate, and dared the precipices and bends in the no-street-lights dead of night, past Pops' and into the bowels of Hillside where Bundy lived. All so Mumfort Taylor could relieve Bundy of his half-assed duties, and perhaps more accurate, relieve his own conscience. I swore, though as a child of God I ought not to, that Mumfort's bang on Bundy's door reverberated in all of Jamaica. I often wondered if the banging wasn't felt in New York. Yes, Mumfort Taylor banged on Bundy's door at some ungodly hour, not neighborly as far as that went. I pictured Bundy on the other side of the wooden door wondering what the hell the police were doing at his house at nearly two in the morning.

Mumfort's luck was uncanny. Or was it his timing? Bundy was amenable to opening his door, perhaps still trying to shake the shackles of drunkenness, even at such impolite time. Bundy was tired, just tired. Somehow I could tell the difference between drunken stupor and fatigue. His eyes were red and swollen, but he opened them, and kept them open without much difficulty.

"A wah wrong now? A late ennuh."

Translation: "What's wrong now? It's late, don't you know."

Meaning: What in God's name could be so urgent, so important you had to rouse me *now*? What was it that could not have waited till day cloud cut, revealing all that is to be to all with eyes?

"I'm Uncle Mumfort," said the man in the ill-fitting clothes that destroyed my image of a foreigner, all the while with his right hand stretched waiting for Bundy to grasp it.

'Uncle Mumfort?' What the hell, who in God's name would call *himself* Uncle?' I thought.

"Diana (few people other than her parents and siblings called my mother Diana) and I…"

Bundy cleared his throat as if preparing his ears for what followed.

"Diana and I are here to tell you that I AM Julie's father, not you. From now on, I'm her father. I am here now, and I'm her father. Me, Uncle Mumfort…

"Bundy…"

"Bundy… You hear me? Bundy…

"Like I was saying, Julie is mine, not yours. Have a good night ol' buddy."

Mumfort again stretched his right hand toward Bundy, only that time he hadn't waited long enough for Bundy to decipher what to do with the outstretched hand.

"Take care now Bundy ol' buddy."

My mother hadn't said a word.

Just like that, Daze was no longer my cousin. Nor was her sister Daphne or brother Mark. None of those people should matter anymore. They were instantly relieved of their familial expectations. And with not so much of a 'thank you' from Mumfort or 'I'm sorry from my mother' Bundy was officially excused from fatherhood.

Before Bundy had time to digest the unpleasantness of conspiring old lovers, my name was changed to Julie Marie Taylor, daughter of Mumfort C. Taylor, stepdaughter of Olga E. Taylor. Daze and her ilk were to be traded for Winston and his. I had new cousins, new aunts, uncles; you get the picture. Sandra and Marcia were to be what Daze was to me, before the betrayal. New family ties meant my good Uncle Verdel's wife, my aunt by marriage, was now my cousin by blood. Process overload. I even inherited a new sister named Blossom Palmer. Like me, she was new to Mumfort, or Mumfort to her. Anyway, Miss Palmer, as she was known, lived in Chapelton, Clarendon and was the owner of a small shop. She sold everything from bun & cheese to flour, a regular little shop. Pleasant enough. I'd soon be visiting my new sister, bringing my 'real' sister Mawma with me. After all, she was my mother's child and couldn't just be taken from me on the word of some strange man who called himself 'uncle.' Familial familiarity. Mumfort was hell bent on introducing his newly claimed bastards, for whatever the reason, to each other.

I had suspected that the aging process was not kind to Mumfort, and that he wanted to ease his conscience before he was relieved of all abilities to remember or remedy. Whatever, at least Miss Palmer had bun & cheese and ice cream cake and ice cream and all kinds of things for which Mawma and I didn't have to shell out one red cent. I found out the first night of our weeklong visit that I was lactose intolerant, you know, prone to diarrhea, you know, belly run when I ingested dairy products. That was new to me because I'd been ingesting fresh from the udder milk with the crème on top forever and never had a reaction. I guessed when you ingest a month's worth of anything in one day it's bound to find a way out of your body. My new sister didn't take too kindly to me blaming her cat for the 'mess.' But then she confessed that dairy didn't agree with her either. Phew, we had something in common other than the moles that apparently most decidedly meant we were of Mumfort. Her mole was unattractive though, big, pronounced and really should have been charged rent for occupying so much of her top lip.

It was proud in its prominence. You saw the mole, then the not-so-bad-looking woman behind the mole. Not like mine, discrete, one neatly on the outer edge of my left cheek and the other hidden from view, unless of course, you were to hoist my dress. My moles were beauty marks. Hers, a mark that made me wonder how her husband and children kept from laughing as the mole moved up and down when Miss Palmer ate or talked or laughed.

I wondered if her nicknames included guacamole?

✝ ✝ ✝

Thus saith the Lord,
Learn not the way of the heathen, and
Be not dismayed at the signs of heaven;
For the heathen are dismayed at them.

—Jeremiah 10:2

My newly acquired cousin, Winston Black, became my new best friend, despite the age difference. He was one of my mother's best friends when they were running around Hillside as kids. He was in his forties, I was in my teens, and that got people talking. They'd talk anyway, about anything. I made it my business to ignore them, their nasty gossip and their predictions. I told myself they were just jealous. After all, I had the cousin with a foreign accent and worldly experience. He, unlike the tongue waggers in Seaforth had live in places most could not even bring their feeble minds to imagine. And he was the one who introduced Bya and I to Silver Slipper and who took us all over the place in the back of his sky-blue pick up truck.

We went to places like Chi-Chi in Morant Bay, the waterfall in White Horses, Bailey's Beach in Yallahs. We went all over the place, like I said, but by far our favorite was just down the road from our house—Silver Slipper. Oh yea, Silver Slipper, Seaforth's first and only discotheque. Stocked with endless rows of Suppligen and Nutrament and Red Stripe and Mr. J Wray & Nephew and Heineken and Guinness and Dragon and Appleton and flashing lights and dark corners the lights couldn't reach and reggae music—sweet, sweet, sweet reggae, music of the devil; not tambourine music that stirred our souls. It was music that made our hips gyrate, music that stirred our soles. It was the same music that blasted from Miss Cherry or Miss Icy bar in which we weren't allowed with the exception of trying to pry a few dollars, or a soda, out of Bundy. It was music that was not some archaic collection of noise and clutter, but sweet music that made us do the Bicycle, the Cool & Deadly, Della Move and too many contortions to list.

What I loved about Winston was that he wasn't afraid. He didn't have to be afraid of God or whoever else would smite him, he had spent decades in America and that somehow had desensitized him to the angry side of God. No, he wouldn't be struck down for going into a place meant for heathens, a den a sin; the devil's breeding ground. He could enjoy the fruits of the flesh without being damned to the pith of hell. He'd always remind us that if Jesus didn't want people to drink alcohol he wouldn't have turned made water into wine. "Why you think He turned water into wine, to wash His feet?" Winston would ask with a self-pleasing grin.

Anyway, my new cousin Winston was fresh, different. Though he was from the parish he was no longer of the parish. We all thought he had spent too many years in New York to be considered a real Jamaican. He was a foreigner. His years away from Jamaica robbed him of his ability to properly speak patois. He understood it though. Kids used to gather to hear him talk. We were sure had he charged an admission fee to the scores gathered to hear him 'twang' and he might have been a millionaire. Winston said things like 'burb,' not belch; thanks not tanks; talk to you later, not awright yuh hear or likkle more; I beg your pardon, not wah yuh seh. To make matters better, Winston's father, the elder Mr. Black was an established and respectable proprietor of all kinds of delights—of the adult or kid variety.

Yes, the elder Mr. Black was one of those men who might have been considered a town sage of sorts, not because he was particularly wise, but because he had stature. He was almost as dignified as Pops, held back only by his choice of profession. See, were the elder Mr. Black not a provider of spirits that promoted promiscuity and other pleasures of the flesh, he might have been considered Pops' equal. But while Pops was busy saving souls, the elder Mr. Black inveigled sin. And unlike Pops, he was a bit of an ugly man really, not ugly but attractive. It could have been as simple as his eyes being too close together, but he had just missed the mark of being handsome. And he had a wayward tongue that he always stuck in any bottle or glass from which he drank. For that we called him Lizzy though in retrospect he was less of a lizard and more of a frog determined to kill a fly in flight. Anyway, despite his tongue, the elder Mr. Black was respected among his kind, and especially by the scores of men and good-for-nothing women he kept sufficiently drunk, from morning till night. His shop was double-sided you could say, one side housed sweets, biscuits, cheese, bun, et cetera; the other side was a bar, yes a rum bar. We loved to visit the sweet side as visits always yielded goodies but had to promise Dee we would absolutely not be caught in the bar. We were not to be mistaken for worthless men or careless women who were almost part of the bar's décor. They were there the minute the doors opened, leaving only upon

closing or when they had sufficiently proved they could no longer sit on the stools, let alone stand.

One such regular was 'boasten-tone' Sarge. Yea, Sarge was
the proud owner of a massive hernia that rivaled the bump of
any belly woman about to piss out someone or other's child.
And his twigs for legs and arms, sunken eyes and bony chest
made him look like someone, on a dare, had crazy glued a boul-
der to his trousers. It just wasn't natural, and I concluded that
if I were as unnatural, I'd drink White Rum from mawning till
miggle night too—without ice, water or any other unnecessary additives. Then I too would let the rum run free from the
lump in the front of my trousers, down my legs before I'd rest
my head on whatever was softer than the bare asphalt: garbage,
dog feces, whatever cushioned the rest.

We were sure all that White Rum kept the stench of urine
and other wastes (human or otherwise) from rising above the
bulge in Sarge's pants and assaulting his nostrils. We smelt
it. Hell, we had to hold our noses and hasten our steps past
where boasten-tone Sarge and his kind spent more nights than
they did with whatever woman unlucky enough to call them
spouse. Drunkie-drunkie Liscom joined Sarge in the cesspool,
but in his defense, that sort of behavior only happened before
he went blind. Somehow he had managed to regain his sight
rumored to have been lost to White Rum. I never quite understood how a man, not unaccustomed to years of hard drinking,
would suddenly go blind then just as suddenly regain his sight.
Miracles abounded, especially for the undeserving. I guessed
God had done for Liscom what He had refused to do for my
dying brother; He chose to return sight to some random old
drunk while He knowingly and with deliberateness, lead my

brother, just 21 years old, to the grave. I guessed for Liscom, wha nuh dead nuh dash weh.

Translation: Don't discard what is not dead.

Meaning: While there's life in even the most undeserving, useless being, there is hope of redemption, of salvation when He has so ordained it.

✝ ✝ ✝

No the serpent was more subtil than any beast of the field which the Lord God had made. And he said unto the woman, Yea, hath God said, Ye shall not eat of every tree of the garden?

—Genesis 3:1

Winston was different, at first. He was kind, gentle and seemed to genuinely care. I had soon learned that what he cared most about was his own urge, an urge that led him to straight my crotch. It was an urge that caused him to put my entire vagina in his mouth. The warmth of saliva on my clitoris was wonderful and weird at the same time. It had felt like the time Monica, Fin's niece, had used her tongue to survey my vagina when I was no older than six or seven. Confusing. Strange. Different. Ecstasy, I imagined. And though you could say I participated, it was a detached participation, like watching myself from *outside* myself.

I might have fully engaged except I knew I shouldn't have Winston's tongue, rabid with curiosity, probing the inner crevices of my vagina. For some bizarre reason though, I had equated his tongue with his father's lizard-like tongue in the bottle. I wondered if the elder Mr. Black's tongue found its way into his wife's vagina, and if she had gotten used to it. Whatever the case, *I* had known better than to enjoy the strange sensation when he took my entire clitoris in his mouth and tossed his head from side to side.

Naturally I questioned God, I questioned my judgment, I questioned why I was scared and overjoyed at the same time. I questioned what it was in me that sent signaled my approval to be fucked by family, and by those posing as caring, loving, protecting, helpful beings. Then I questioned the validity of what I had felt with Winston's tongue in me; was it really wrong to feel scared—and stirred all at the same time? I didn't have to question what would come next; I simply could not afford to carry on being stuck in weird. The solution was simple: I wasn't going to repeat the offense. I didn't want to be one of those girls who *willingly* gave themselves to their relatives; even newly acquired blood ought not to mingle.

I never went back to visit Winston, not even on the promises of goodies and Sunday afternoon excursions. Like everyone before him, Winston simply didn't respect the lines drawn in blood; no matter how fresh or newly discovered the blood. And so the first time became the last time, and for what it was worth, I didn't even bother telling Dee, I felt too much shame. Or was it that she would have said 'that's what you get for spending so much time with someone old enough to be your father?' It was just easier to disconnect, to block the opportunity to ever have my clitoris in Winston's mouth again—and better, bury the memory of it having happened in the first place.

✠ ✠ ✠

For this ye know, that no whoremonger, nor unclean person, nor covetous man, who is an idolater, hath any inheritance in the kingdom of Christ and of God. Let no man deceive you with vain words: because of these things cometh the wrath of God upon the children of disobedience. Be not ye therefore partakers with them. For ye were sometimes darkness, but now light in the Lord: walk as children of light: For the fruit of the Spirit [is] in all goodness and righteous, Proving what is acceptable unto the Lord. And have no fellowship with the unfruitful works of darkness, but rather reprove [them] for it is a shame even to speak of those things which are done of them in secret. But all things that are reproved are made manifest by the light: for whatsoever doth make manifest is light. Wherefore he saith, Awake thou that sleepest, and Arise from the dead, and Christ

shall give thee light. See then that ye walk circumspectly, not as fools, but as wise, redeeming the time, because the days are evil. Wherefore be ye not unwise, But understanding what the will of the Lord, and be not drunk with wine, wherein is excess; but be filled with the Spirit.

—Ephesians 5:5-18

It had been nearly two years since Oin left and some years since they had all had their way with me: from the uncle to the cousin to the church brother to the obeah man. I was done with Morant Bay High School, had tried nursing school, but having never figured out why I needed to become the nurse and not the doctor, I couldn't be bothered with that either. I did little to advance my life, and lots to destroy it. My mother was overjoyed when her brother Norburt returned from New York to announce he was taking me back with him. He did not consult, he announced with resolute confidence that Dee would not object or even question. She didn't.

I knew I would miss my familiar terribly, but was determined to go in search of my dreams. Folks always said, "dreams don't chase you, you better get off your ass and chase your them." Besides something had to be done with my life and apparently it had to be done straight away, no tarrying. Norburt and I left in quite the hurry. Like a thief in the night, we left for Montego Bay where, rather than go straight to the airport, as I had assumed, he checked us into some fancy hotel where the local currency was fake shark's teeth worn on a string around the neck; picture being leid without the flowers. I didn't ask questions, I simply did what Norburt did. He was my uncle who lived in New York, well heeled, revered by the family. And *he* had chosen to do something with *my* life.

Ever the considerate uncle, Norburt had brought me a suitcase of foreign clothes so I looked like one of them. I blended in and no one asked what this local girl was doing with that foreign man. We spent the day doing what tourists did: lay by the pool, drink, eat, drink some more, frolic in the beach, drink some more, shower, eat again, drink some more. I had imagined that was what they did, anyways. I'd never had a drink with rum in it before, and the first one took me by surprise. I immediately thought back to Drunkie-drunkie Liscom and Bundy and their kind, and wondered why and how they couldn't live a day without white rum. I drank the rum-accompanied drink to show my uncle that I could be one of them. Just as I was getting tolerant of the rum-accompanied drink though, Norburt ordered a different drink, something far fancier looking with slices of pineapple and a little umbrella sticking out. I had never seen anything like it before, not even on TV, and knew Mawma would be as tickled as I was so I kept the little umbrella with all intentions of sending it back to her once I arrived in Brooklyn, New York. See, all our toys were made by us, and I knew she'd enjoyed a real toy, not an empty Pepsi bottle in which we crammed a wad of grass meant to be hair, or the empty Sudsil or Fab detergent box converted into a doll's bed, or an empty juice box stuffed with paper so we could play baseball. Handmade toys; nothing else quite inspired hours of unadulterated fun without worrying about breaking some store-bought sterile toy, that were we lucky enough to get one by whatever means. And besides, any real toy would have immediately joined the mish mash figurines meant to decorate our house. I still remember back in 1974, when my mother's sister Sophia came visiting from London. She had bought me a purple teddy bear that I had no time to even acquaint myself with its makeup. My hands were barely around it when Dee took it for safekeeping, aka, accessory to her décor. I was allowed to admire it. I was never allowed to touch it.

Anyway, back to the fancy drink with the pretty, pretty umbrella and pineapple. We had spent the entire day doing what I imagined *all* foreigners did—we lollygagged. We had done nothing all day, and frankly I was a bit glad when day started turning to evening. Though I was born and raised in Jamaica, I'd never much paid attention to sunsets. They were so mechanical, so expected, so had nothing to do with me. Suddenly there we were, Norburt and I sat sitting in watch as the sun turned colors, all shades of red and orange and plum and even brown, as it sank from the sky and fell into the water. There were fewer stars than we had in Seaforth, more electricity but far fewer stars. And drunken white people staggered about, much like Drunkie-drunkie Liscom and Bundy. On the dance floor, they flailed like flounders out of water, and they spoke with weird accents like the ones we heard on TV. I danced like freedom. At least I didn't have to worry about Dee tapping me on the shoulder and shaming me into returning to church where all decent young ladies danced in the prescribed manner.

I danced to reggae, I danced to calypso; I even danced to soul music. And I drank between dances not paying much attention to how exaggerated each drink made my Della Move or my Bicycle. When we finally got back to the room with two beds, I sank into the one closest to the door and tried to close my eyes. But closing my eyes only made the bed spin violently, as if to evict my drunken body. So I opened my eyes wide, deliberately wide, and stared at the popcorn ceiling (I'd never seen anything so fancy). That slowed the bed some. Before long though, I had to rush into the bathroom as the contents of my stomach made a beeline for my throat. I vomited an orange-brown concoction I didn't remember eating. But at least I felt better; not well, better. I rinsed my mouth and returned to bed, with determinedly open eyes. I stared again at the ceiling and tried to count all the popcorn.

Norburt leaned over me and mumbled something I thought was 'are you okay?' If I were okay it would not have been for much longer. Just as George had done nearly a decade earlier, Norburt raised my dress and lowered my panties. I didn't try to fight, I didn't try to scream, I didn't try to run. Where was I to run in that strange, foreign part of my not-so-everyday Jamaica?

I just remained there while my soul seeped out of my body. I just laid there, unfortunately alive, alert and sobered by the "act." I was sober but soulless as my mother's brother thrust his penis in and out of my vagina. I didn't think. I didn't react. My soul floated above and watched my uncle remove himself from my body. I was too uncaring to move. The following day, May 24, 1986, we checked out of the hotel with enough time to ease to Sangster International Airport.

I'd only ever seen the outside of Norman Manley International Airport, Jamaica's only other airport. I had even been to its waving gallery sometimes. Yes, NMIA had a waving gallery where relatives and friends went to wave as their loved ones board whatever plane headed to wherever they thought better than Jamaica. But *I* was a traveler on May 24, 1986, and would be permitted beyond the point where I'd used to stand and imagine 'one day' that'll be me.

My one-day I'll go to 'foreign' had come. Norburt gave me my travel documents and I sat in silence and stared through them, knowing that at least I will be leaving the bowels of Seaforth and wouldn't have to tell Dee that her revered brother had penetrated me. Not that she would have been particularly perturbed, I supposed. 'At least,' she might have thought, 'a better life awaited my Julie.'

I wasn't hungry or thirsty or questioning. I just sat and stared and felt the emptiness grow. I was a shell too unclean for a soul. When thoughts and feelings returned, I hoped there were strong enough to soothe, to wrap me in reassurance that everything was going to be just fine, and that Norburt had only temporarily lost his decency to the evils of intoxication, he had simply lost his compass for a minute; he was not like George. But any soothing affirmation was killed by the reality of my situation.

Unfortunately the promise of my new life grew increasingly suffocating as reality became real; no retreating to Seaforth, only going forward to do something with my life, chase a dream that had just began with a nightmare...

✝ ✝ ✝

Go your ways: behold I send you forth as lambs among wolves. Carry neither purse, nor scrip, nor shoes: and salute no man by the way. And in whatsoever city ye enter, and they receive you, eat such things as are set before you: and heal the sick that are therein, and say unto them, The kingdom of God is come nigh unto you. But into whatsoever city ye enter, and they receive you not, go your ways out into the streets of the same and say, even the very dust of your city, which cleaveth on us, we do wipe off against you: Notwithstanding be ye sure of this, that the kingdom of God is come nigh unto you. But I say unto you, that it shall be more tolerable in that day for Sodom, than for that city.

—Luke 10:3-12

The plane landed scarcely an hour after it had taken off. I was still taking mental photographs of the strange seats with seat belts and the narrow aisle and the strange tray on which we had to eat. It was all so alien and though I wanted to pee so badly, I refused to try and figure out how to use the bathroom, if indeed there was one. Buses didn't have toilets so why should airplanes? I convinced myself there weren't any toilets. After all, they couldn't just flush the mess over people's heads, or so I thought. I buried the urgency of wanting, no needing to go the bathroom. I'd become expert at burying: desires, needs, wants, occurrences, episodes. Just bury.

I wondered why I couldn't sit next to my uncle, because though I couldn't look at him, at least he'd been on airplanes dozens of times before, and could have given me a tutorial on how to fasten my seat belt, hell he could have told me what a seat belt was, or explain its usefulness. I wondered if his presence, his being closer would have comforted or incensed. He was after all a pedophile rapist, but he was familiar, he was family, taking me from the pits of Seaforth to the land of abounding opportunities.

Then I remembered I was frightened—not illiterate. Unlike the scores of people left back in Seaforth, I could read and therefore had the wherewithal to follow the instructions on the seat belt. And despite my predicament, I still remembered his address for the form I had to complete. I'd written dozens, if not hundreds of letters to the same address, asking for money for this, that and the other. It was to be my address in a few hours, and soon people would write to me there asking me for money for this, that and the other. Before long I would be getting letters addressed to Miss Julie Taylor, not to Seaforth Post Office but to Brooklyn, New York, USA. Letters that would start, 'Dear Julie, I hope this letter finds you in the best of health…' But we still had to disembark and clear immigration and custom. So very foreign, I thought. I followed the herd of people and did what they did. I dared not deviate and though the urgency to pee had returned, I was too shy, or perhaps too overwhelmed, to ask for a bathroom.

I wondered why Norburt stayed steps behind me. Maybe shame kept him afar. Or guilt. It might even have been remorse.

It was my turn with the Immigration officer but before I could answer his questions, my bladder acquiesced to nerves and sent pee rushing down my new black jeans and into my new white Keds. I was shown to the bathroom without having to ask, and chuckled at the thought of the people behind me having to do some fancy dance to avoid stepping in my pee.

We took a taxi, just the two of us, not throngs of people piling in, and no young girl sitting with a gear stick between her legs. No, it was just the two of us, my uncle and I, in the *back* seat. I sat as far as possible, leaning on the door of the taxi, ensuring enough space between my uncle and I. I sat with my

back toward him and my face peeled to the window, partly
because I didn't want to accidentally catch my uncle's gaze,
partly to register what I was seeing for the first time. I thought
about the strangeness of foreign. I was amazed at the number
of taxis, and that they all looked alike, no personalization, no
names. America, at least that part of America had huge streets,
free of potholes and had far too many traffic lights to try and
memorize where to turn. Yes, I was amazed at the streets, I'd
seen them in movies, but it was still strange to see three lanes
in *one* direction.

Ugly brown houses were everywhere and I wondered why
someone didn't paint them. I was amazed at the number of
cars—and all the different types.

I wondered if my uncle and the taxi driver could smell my
pee. I wondered if anyone had ever peed in front of immigration officers before. I wondered if my Dee and Fin and Bya and
Mawma and Stephanie missed me, and if they were crying. I
wondered how long it would be before I would see them again.
What was Norburt's wife like? What did his house look like? I
hoped it had color, vibrancy; you know, life. The taxi stopped
in front a long row of ugly brick buildings. I wondered whom
Norburt knew in prison. Without laboring to try and catch,
let alone hold each other's gaze, we exchanged our first words
since the "act."

"We're here. Come, let's go."

"Where are we going?" I mumbled more than asked.

"This is where I live," he said without so much as a tinge of
shame for what he had done to me the night before. There was
nothing in his voice to say 'I'm sorry I got carried away with all
that drinking, and what you were wearing, though I'd brought

it for you, didn't help.' There was nothing to say anything outside *his* norm had happened mere hours before.

"How do you know which one is yours, they all look alike?"

"Because this is where I live, this is my house."

"How come they are all joined?"

"Because that's how they're built."

"Aren't you afraid people can hear all your business?"

"Everybody mind them own business," he said with a certain confidence in his tone, one meant to tell me that unless *I* told, no one would know.

No one was nosy enough to go poking around in other people's affairs. That was devastating because all along I clung to the hope that things were different in America, and that had someone found out what my uncle had done and be nosy enough to share with the police, something would be done; my uncle would be held responsible for taking what wasn't his, just as he was guilty of taking what was his—flesh of his sister's child.

I cried. I wasn't sure why I was crying, but I couldn't stop. I didn't stop when Norburt's wife Marcia came and said hello. She must have thought me strange. I cried when her daughter Sally said hello. And when Zack, Norburt and Marcia's son said hello I cried. I bawled when Norburt's niece, my cousin Joycelin hugged me. I didn't stop crying for the parade of people, relatives I'd never known, in a strange house. I could have been crying because I missed my familiar of Dee and Fin and Bya and Stephanie and Mawma.

I could have been crying because I'd not quite buried the 'act' of Norburt penetrating me, fresh burial needed time to set. I could have been crying for fear I'd never find the house again were I brave enough to venture outside. The houses were the same. The streets were the same. There were no big ackee trees for markers. I could have been crying because I thought everyone knew I'd peed in my new black jeans and white Keds, and would think *I* was strange. I could have been crying because "everybody mind them own business" in this strange house. I could have been crying at the thought of my uncle fucking me AND everyone in the strange house: his wife, his other niece, his stepdaughter.

I just cried, and it felt good, cleansing almost. And somehow I had expected that once the tears stopped, so would the aching to see Dee and Fin and Bya and Mawma and Stephanie. The urgent need to be back home in Seaforth became unbearable. As bad as things were back in my part of Jamaica, I always knew my way back home. I knew that even in the dead of night, I could always see where I was going, even if I didn't always get there without deviations—planned or spontaneous. I missed the big ackee tree. I missed the post office. I missed the rows of apple trees that gave the path to our house its name: Apple Lane.

I missed the familiarity of just knowing what to expect, mostly. I really missed my family; I knew them and they knew me. I didn't know the strange people with whom I'd be sharing a house. I didn't see how I was to have done something with my life in such a foreign place. I was alone and lonely and sad and dirty and disgusting and soiled in a house full of people, apparently my people.

Naturally, I started thinking of all the things I should have done to Norburt, and the things I should have said to him. I thought I should have had the courage to say, "this is my life and you can't fuck it up." I should have refused his kindness to rescue me from the life of uncertainty Seaforth held for me. I thought it bizarre that even if Seaforth had little to offer someone like me, I would have been better off taking my chances, with that uncertainty than be plagued by the certainties of my new future.

After the first dinner in my new home, I withdrew into myself to mourn in private. I closed my eyes and squeezed them as tightly as I could, all so I could make sure the faces of my parents and siblings would be seared onto my brain. It was all to make sure I would never forget them or their quirks, like the way Dee always stuck her tongue to the side when she tried to concentrate, or the way Fin's eyes twinkled when he tried to smile. I had no physical photographs and had to rely on flashbacks.

Marcia was an OR nurse. She was kind, very kind. Nurturing. No wonder she was a nurse, an educated, highly specialized Jamaican transplant. And she was Norburt's wife. She complemented him, at least physically. If he was handsome, she was stunning, gorgeous, woman, always impeccably dressed, and with almost white skin, green eyes and almost-blond hair, I imagined all the women hated her; they certainly would have back in Seaforth. I was proud she was my aunt, and that she took me shopping and welcomed me to her home, despite her and my uncle being on the brink of divorce. Sure they lived in the same house. Apparently American laws were as strange as its houses. They stayed living together because the first person to move out of the house would have lost it to other with more perseverance, more greed. So they both stayed, staking claim to the strange house. The wife on the top floors, the husband in the basement, albeit a finished basement. The arrangement might have been odd but at least they weren't feuding. In fact, other than not sharing a marital bed, they behaved every bit like the happily married couple: she cooked his food, laundered his clothes, cared for his nieces, et cetera.

For bed sharing, Norburt had Rita, a snow-white Italian-American woman with three daughters: Lisette, Felicia and Lindsay. I'd met Rita when she accompanied Norburt to Jamaica, and had mistakenly thought *she* was his wife. She had even brought me the sphygmomanometer and other necessaries for nursing school. Anyway, Rita lived a few minutes away, in Canarsie, the all-white-no-black-families section of Brooklyn. She was Norburt's concubine, in the biblical sense, and I thought it strange that their adulterous relationship didn't keep Pops and Mama from denouncing their son. Hell, they made my good Uncle Verdel marry his girlfriend before night could catch her at the house that Pops built. They had made George do the same, though they did nothing to stop him from fucking family. And remember they had rented a house for Diana so her out-of-wedlock pregnancy wouldn't reflect too glaringly on them. Age must have mellowed my grandparents because even though they knew Norburt was still married to Marcia, they didn't mind Rita and Norburt sleeping in the same bed when they visited Jamaica. They hadn't even refused the gifts she had brought them. My grandparents were like that; they shunned anything that contradicted the Word, itself beyond reproach. But they chose to ignore Norburt's trespasses. They had even forgiven him for marrying Marcia upon divorcing Judith, his first wife. Mama and Pops were selective in condemning in the name of the Lord. Relative wealth, or the appearance thereof, and its ability to breed and foster dependency dictated how the Bible and its principles were applied—and to whom.

But alas, time heals all wounds they say, and with the passage of the first few months and with everyone rallying to help acclimate me to the newness of life, I might not have had my familiar, but I was slowly becoming familiar with my new realities. I was a Jamaican living in New York, under the stewardship of an uncle who afforded me the opportunity to do something with my life; with his wife who treated me with uncommon and unwarranted kindness; with his concubine who treated me well enough to further endear herself to him. I remember her taking me to the doctor when I couldn't shake the pain in my lower belly. The doctor had apparently told her, not me, it was as a result of *all* my sexual partners. I wondered if she knew her adulterous lover was one of them. There were injections to cure whatever ailed my cervix, nothing to heal my soul.

In any event, life was good, not great because I still missed my familiar. I still cried for them, and for me. But I had found a job as a receptionist, was saving money—me saving money, and had before long sent one container with shoes and food (of course only non-perishables) and clothes and toys, real toys, and peas and towels, etc. A second container was already half-full and though I often got lost navigating the streets of New York, I had learned how to minimize the associated stress. I was doing well. I was being left alone to flourish, to breathe without panting, without tentacles constantly trying to rip my clothes to pieces, to rip my soul to shreds. I was free to be Julie, a teenage girl with all the crushes and discoveries and 'normal' angst.

✣ ✣ ✣

And in the same house remain, eating and drinking such things as they give: For the labourer is worthy of his hire. Go not from house to house.

—Luke 10:7

Freedom had seldom been more fleeting. After months of living without fear of Norburt's affection, I suddenly became the target body, the receptacle for his 'love.' His concubine wasn't enough to satisfy his urges so he went after me—again and again and again. Brooklyn was becoming my hell; my uncle's brick house my prison not unlike the brick-enclosed pens that kept the *known* scum of Jamaica confined to their fate. I plotted my escape, but what would I do, where would I go. I'd never considered Mumfort Taylor an ally. I just never considered him. And though two other uncles lived in Brooklyn, one was on drugs and unpredictable; the other, Junior lived in an undesirable neighborhood, or so I'd been taught.

Junior, the uncle who had been my favorite had migrated to the US and was living on Rutland Road and East 94th Street—not a respectable or particularly safe part of town Norburt would often say. "I don't know why dem choose fi live like that," he would lament, to which I'd wondered, 'live like what?' I guessed Norburt condemned Junior for not living up to the example set by him, an older, wiser brother. No, Junior didn't fuck his nieces and stepdaughters. Junior preferred the ease of a life free of pretenses. He might have lived in the undesirable part of Brooklyn but at least he wasn't a savage who hid behind pomp. He chose decency, and raised his beloved Cassandra and Brandon with an undying real love, not a show to meet expectations, but real honest parental love and protection.

Just as Junior was an enviable father, he was the quintessential uncle. Not particularly big for a Montgomery, he was rail thin and always felt more comfortable behind a full beard. He had had his jaw broken twice, and his jaw being sewn shut meant all his meals had to be had through a straw. Needless to say that episode had made us worry he would all but disappear. He hadn't an ounce to spare. Lucky for us, there were all kinds of roots and bushes and Irish moss to fatten, or at least keep my uncle from becoming the invisible man. Junior would twice emerge from a broken jaw a few pounds lighter but no less ready to defend his honor, or that of those he loved. Only death could keep him from fighting for what he knew was right. He might have been quick to fight but he was just as kind and generous and caring and loving. When he left for America in 1982, I had felt the loss of being called Baby Girl. Baby Girl was perhaps the only term of endearment, of affection I can recall from childhood, that, and Mother Speck. Yea, Junior either called me Baby Girl or Mother Speck. I called him Winky. Not that I was unique in calling him Winky, that's what everyone called him; even Cassandra and Brandon. I had missed the 'name callings.'

When I was again reunited with my Uncle Junior, I visited every chance. My Uncle Junior treated me as his third child. I relished the trips to Coney Island or the beach or Kings Plaza mall. I missed people's gasps as Junior, all 300-plus pounds of his girlfriend Beuhla, Cassandra, Brandon, Beuhla's kids Yvette, Dennis and Eric—and myself would climb out of Junior's two-door Honda hatchback meant for four people not too concerned with comfort or luxury.

What Junior did for and to his children and stepchildren, he did to and for me: he showered us with love and kindness and care and protection and allowances. But he lived in the 90s, as that part of Brooklyn was known; that part that could have easily been mistaken for Rema or Jungle back in Jamaica. The sounds of gunshots were sometimes as common as the sounds of fire-crackers on July 4th.

On a warm June evening, I didn't care about random gunshots or bustled streets. I'd had enough of Norburt, and though my departure might have been hastened, I was glad it had finally come. Salvation was at hand. Somehow Winsome, my aunt, found out that I was Norburt's available and convenient way to satisfy his urge for incestuous sex.

I was relieved someone had finally realized Norburt was more monstrous than Freddie Kruger, a wholly fictionalized character. I was ecstatic Winsome had made the gruesome discovery; it meant I'd be saved, freed. If Norburt was the respected male member of the Montgomery clan, Winsome was his revered female counterpart. She was the sensible, successful sibling. She was beautiful and soft spoken and I often fantasized she was my mother forced to hand me over to the older sister so as not to cause too much shame on the clan. We looked alike. But I also looked like my mother and my aunts and my uncles. We all looked alike.

In any event, Winsome, my mother-aunt was going to be my savior. Until, that is, the shame and shock of a discovery

so gruesome made her sensibilities take flight (if but temporary). She pointed the finger at me, literally, in a wrist flicking
motion that made her index finger move back and forth as it
jerked with fury, with rebuke, but not at her brother. The disgust was assigned to me; it was my fault for bringing shame to
her brother, to her family.

"Look what you did!" she scolded.

"You, you, you, have brought shame on the only respectable one. You are a dirty little girl." I suspected she was too
disappointed in her brother, too shocked to point the finger
in the right direction. I had almost understood that she was
blinded to the truth. Hell, *it* was happening to me and could
hardly believe it myself.

"What were you thinking? My God, what have you done?"
she continued to berate. Thankfully the questions were rhe-
torical because I could not formulate a response.

Norburt, predator in pause, stood there, head hung low
as his sister gave me, his prey a verbal lashing, worse than
any physical beatings I'd endured at my mother's hands. At
least it felt that way. Years of physical blows may have left
scars; the words just ricocheted in my head with no way of
escaping. And, in a weird way Dee's beatings were forgiv-
able, I knew she meant well, she just had the worst way of
showing it. In fact, I was sure the beatings were my mother's
way of loving, caring and protecting. I somehow expected my
aunt to provide words of comfort and reassurance that, like
Bob Marley sang, every likkle ting gonna be alright. I didn't
expect Norburt to come to my defense. I didn't expect him
to assume the blame. I didn't expect him to reject the absolu-
tion Winsome bestowed on him.

Norburt just stood in silent agreement with his sister. He said nothing. The gig was up but though *I* had tarnished *his* image, though not outside the boundaries of repair; his yielding to temptation was deserving of forgiveness. His penance would make him whole again: a few altruistic gestures—send some money to the parents and siblings back in Jamaica, give the old car to a relative in need, or any such charity—would ensure his light once again shine, halo intact.

I was the pariah; the misfit assigned the scarlet letter. At 17, I was the black widow whose venom had taken away Norburt's ability to speak, to declare his weakness and beg forgiveness. To keep my head from exploding into a million insignificant pieces, I held it under the cold running water in Norburt's subterranean kitchen. I just let the water run on my head, not thinking or caring that it would mean a trip back to the hairdresser. The water wasn't for cleansing, I'd learned that didn't work; it was to keep me from going crazy, to quiet the chorus of chaos, to keep all the once-buried memories from rushing through my skull in a stampede to escape this 'dirty little girl.'

Drenching my head was all I could do amidst the snot and tears. I couldn't speak. I couldn't form words, just images of Dee and George and Norburt and Bushy and Brother Jeremiah Truman. I couldn't say, "but Aunty Winsome, he…"

I could run, though. I wasn't held captive by a dying brother's condition and my obligation to submit to whatever, whomever promised to restore him. Nor were my feet paralyzed by fear as they had been on the path with George. They might have even been fueled by fear if you ask me. I ran. I ran, hair dripping, tears flowing, snot running. I ran like a wild beast just freed from a cage meant to tame it. I ran from East 57th Street, down Farragut, across the strange streets with prison facades to nowhere in particular. I stopped running on Ralph Avenue and Farragut Road, just by the bus stop. A car full of young white men shrouded in strangeness stopped and offered me a ride. They saw my distress. Or was it my vulnerability? The inner voice that told me to run also told me to decline the offer.

I waited and sobbed and wondered, and I yearned for peace.

I wondered why my uncles were given freedom and approval to fuck me and managed to make me the 'dirty little girl.' I thought about the time when Pops told Dee and Fin to "tek you lickle dutty liad gyal outta mi yard." I wondered what *I* emanated; what was it in my aura that told my uncles it was okay for them to fuck me; what was it in me that said I was receptive; what said I was a temptress? Then I thought that if I was emanating desire or provocation, my cousins must have been too. The only difference was that they were mostly attracting their own fathers.

My uncle Roxley was fucking his daughters too. Samantha, his second of four girls borne by Marybeth, was perhaps reconciled with her fate of being her father's lover. She had even accepted that her sisters were co-lovers. But when her father began inquiring about the youngest, Latoya, Samantha had had enough. At least one of the four siblings should be spared the affections of a rogue father.

A father's inquiries into his youngest child's menstruation schedule was simply too much. It became the proverbial straw to the camel. Samantha summoned the courage and reported her father to the police. Roxley was arrested. But before the case was brought to trial, Samantha, the complainant, was quite literally removed from the island, not for her safety and wellbeing, but simply and deliberately to save a family name, to keep family matters, no matter how cancerous, within the family. Who in God's name would want such laundry paraded in front of a judge and jury perhaps themselves the target of complaining daughters. Judge not that ye be not judged, right?

In any event, 'The People' couldn't proceed against Roxley. The evidence had been removed; she had been brought to Bermuda. Once the case was resolved in Roxley's favor, resulting in his release and full dismissal of the charges, Samantha was returned to her father in Jamaica. But at least Marybeth had the good sense to take her daughters, apparently too much of a temptation for a father with wayward attraction, and return to her own people. The only consolation was that Roxley had spent *some* time, mere months behind bars awaiting materialization of the evidence against him. At least he felt the confinement of a prison to which he had sentenced his children with the harshest of punishments: life without parole. Fleeting though it was, we hoped Roxley's time away from society was at least long enough for him to see the wrong in him sticking his penis in his daughters' vaginas—and enjoying it.

Then there was poor Gabby, another cousin whose mother had left her in the care of Stephen, Gabby's father and her mother's physical abuser. On its own that was not altogether bad, except Stephen's care of his daughter was more conjugal in nature. Gabby took the place of her mother as far as Stephen was concerned, in every way possible. She endured the beatings and the bed sharing.

No one knew, or maybe everyone knew and no one said anything, no one did anything. Gabby must have thought she struck pure gold when she was brought to Bermuda. Her luck was short lived though, because not unlike Hoggybus' dog, Gabby didn't know how to comport herself. She was far too promiscuous and uncouth, and cast an unwelcome shadow. And just like that, Gabby was back in the care of her father and all his incestuous tendencies. The night before Gabby was to return to Jamaica, she couldn't stop projectile vomiting. She hadn't said why her guts were trying to escape her body; she just couldn't stop vomiting. It was only after father and daughter were reunited that everyone found out, irrefutably, that Gabby was her father's recipient of that kind of love. Years later Gabby ended up in prison, a real physical one that is, for attempted murder, not of her father but some poor defenseless man who had never done anything to warrant that fate. Well, not that we know. Anyway, while out on bail and awaiting trial for that attempted murder, Gabby found herself in yet another legal predicament, only that time with new, separate and far more sinister charges of murder. She was only 21.

I was scarcely surprised Stephen had it in him, and even as everyone wondered how and why, I always knew he had those tendencies. He never physically attacked me; his approach was subtler, more humane. His advances were a little more, well, polite. He tried to seduce; to lure; to bait. He preferred coercion to compulsion, at least where I was concerned. He often said to me, "bwoy Julie mi like you bad. Mi like yuh so much, mi love you."

Translation: Julie I like you desperately. I like you so much I think I love you."

Meaning: If you are open, I would like to get with you. Yea, his approach was a little more polite, less barbaric. He was less of a brute than his youngest sibling George, who just took what he wanted, when he wanted, even from his own daughters when he did have children. (Remind me to tell you about that later.)

But back to Stephen, surely his daughter Gabby was too young to even have an aura, to emit desire. But that had not stopped Stephen from making his daughter his connubial companion. Nothing happened to Stephen. In any event, I have never stopped wondering about another cousin, Karla, my good Uncle Verdel's daughter.

Verdel had left for America back in 1980, leaving his four children with Mama and Pops. Roxley, Stephen and George, despite being grown men, still lived with their parents—and with Verdel's kids. Karla was the eldest and the only girl. She was left in the den with Roxley, Stephen and George—never an easier or more helpless and convenient prey for uncles with no limits on their sexual appetites. A fatherless girl was just the sort of attraction for our uncles. Hell, I was sure neither Roxley nor Stephen nor George gave a second thought to what it might feel like if Roxley fucked Stephen's daughter, or George fucked Roxley's or any weird combination of incest. I was sure they knew of each other's dirty little urges, well not so little to their victims, and I was more sure each one did everything to protect the other, stand guard if you will to the secret of sex among the Montgomerys. I wondered if our uncles ever had Karla all at once in some sick orgy or if they had arrangements, designated nights.

✞ ✞ ✞

Be sober, be vigilant; because your adversary the devil, as a roaring lion, walketh about, seeking whom he may devour.

—1 Peter 5:8

would have been a fool to not think about Karla. Given the history and frequency of abuse, it wasn't odd of me to wonder. It would have been odd not to wonder. Look what happened to Tiffany, Rose's baby? Tiffany is yet another cousin who survived. You'll have to forgive me; Pops and Mama had 73 grandchildren, lots to recall, to lament experiences at the hands of Montgomery boys behaving abhorrently.

Tiffany was 10 years old when her father summoned her from Jamaica to London. She, one of George's many children with as many women, had been abandoned by her own mother Rose, and was being raised by Rose's mother.

Like me so many before her, Tiffany had hardly been outside the district limits, let alone been on a plane. Needless to say, she was happy to be *wanted* by her father since she had never known her mother.

Tiffany found London to be different. Not necessarily better, just different. She had inherited an instant family of older and younger siblings: Devonte and Paloma were from George's first marriage to Nicole; Khadija was from his current wife Suzanne. Suzanne herself had brought a son Lewis into the marriage. Instantly, Tiffany found herself surrounded by love and family—not just a grandmother forced to care. There was affection, real affection, especially between her younger sister and her father, George. There were hugs and horseplay, and the open display of love made Tiffany giddy with hope.

"I just loved the way my dad was with the kids," Tiffany recalled. "And especially with Khadija."

It was a relationship Tiffany wanted for herself, in part to make up for the years without her father; in part to reconcile how a mother, especially one named Rose could simply abandon her. Tiffany had fast become part of the unit, and was subject to the same rules and regulations—and the same privileges. And there were lots of privileges, but perhaps the most antici-pated were birthdays. They were special and because they were special, the birthday boy or girl got to stay home from school. On her 11th birthday, she had done just that, stayed home to do absolutely nothing.

Or so Tiffany had thought.

She spent the day fighting her father—not fighting with, fighting off. It was most definitely not the kind of verbal volley borne out of a disappointment in receiving a less than perfect or expected birthday gift. It was a much more life altering fight.

"I was so happy when my dad let me jump on his lap. I mean I was just giggling so much. Until all of a sudden I felt him grinding on my bum." Tiffany was stoic and matter of fact in her recollection. Even those of us living in America had heard rumblings of what George had done to his daughter. For me though, there was far too much chatter about Tiffany yet no one was talking to her. I reached out to my cousin and told her of my own experiences before asking if she wanted to talk about hers. I wanted her to know she was not alone. She had hesitated none.

"He what?" I asked, not sure if what I was surprised or disappointed in what Tiffany was saying. I had long wished the rumors were just that, rumors.

"Yea, he was just grinding on my bum. I jumped straight off and asked him what he was doing."

"Nothing, what do you mean?" her father had asked.

"You were grinding on my bum dad."

"No I wasn't."

"Dad, I know what I felt, you were grinding on my bum."

That night, after the birthday celebrations had concluded, it was back to the business of everyday life. Tiffany went to bed, on the bottom bunk in the room she shared with Khadija.

"I must have been in bed for about an hour, thinking about what had happened and if I had imagined it. All of a sudden I felt someone hugging me from the back. It was my dad."

Apparently George wanted to erase all doubts in Tiffany's mind. No she wasn't imagining he had been grinding on her.

"My dad was naked on the bottom and put his hand over my mouth. He then used his mouth to cover mine so I wouldn't scream. It was the scariest night of my life. There I was, wondering how I could have even thought that about my dad, and there he was sticking his tongue down my throat. He groped and tried to stick his finger in me. On my birthday! My 11th birthday."

Tiffany had been given the most unenviable of birthday gifts. She was given a life sentence of guilt and shame and promiscuity and abuse and thoughts of suicide. Even at 11, she knew what her father had done was the ultimate treachery, the ultimate sin. She knew instantly she would have been better off with a feeble grandmother than a loving father.

She confronted him a day later.

"Why did you do that to me dad? You know I'm going to tell, right?"

"Little Man told me to do it. He told me to see what you were like with men because you were so big."

"What, you sick fuck?"

"Yea, he said that you have big breasts and a big bum so I should see what you were like with men."

George had said his best friend from childhood suggested then encouraged the attempt on Tiffany. His excuse was original and might even have been funny if the circumstances were different. He claimed his friend had told him Tiffany was quite developed for her age. He claimed his friend told him to find out how Tiffany was with men. He claimed he was asked to 'test-drive' his daughter.

"How can Little Man tell you to fuck your own daughter dad?"

"It's not like there is anything wrong with it, all the Asians do it."

"You're a sick fuck, *dad*. And I'm going to tell."

"Look at me and look at you, who's going to believe you?"

George knew Tiffany was serious about telling, and all the years of his predation would end just like that. He didn't want to risk his daughter being believed. He put Tiffany in the car and drove her to his older brother's house. Ed, Pops and Mama's eldest son had been living in England since the 1950s, but had recently traded the miserable English weather for the Florida sunshine. George was left to watch the house until it was rented or sold. He took Tiffany to the back of Ed's empty house, produced a machete and showed her just where her final resting place would be, were she to tell.

"If you tell nuhbody, I will kill yuh bloodclawt and bury you right here in a Ed's yard. You won't even be missed."

The threat of death was enough to seal Tiffany's mouth. Well, except it was pried open to make way for her father's tongue. He continued groping and grinding and kissing and fingering his daughter. She continued to try and fight, to avoid, to ensure she was rarely left alone in her father's care.

"I would not come home after school until I was sure my stepmom was home."

Then when Leighton, another of George's children (from yet another mother) was brought up from Jamaica to join the family, Tiffany risked her life and confided in her newly added older brother.

"Leighton cried and cried. And then he told me dad would never touch me again, that he would protect me from our father."

At first Leighton said nothing, but he, my brother, did all he could to protect his sister from their father. He then told Devonte, George's first of two children with ex-wife Nicole, and together brothers banded to protect their sister. They took turns sleeping in Tiffany's bed, standing guard against a father, their father. Just as George was determined to violate, the brothers were determined to protect their sister, and though they hadn't the courage to tell what a father, their own, was doing to a daughter, they handled the situation as well as can be expected of a couple teenage boys. George hated that 'his sons took turns in his daughter's bed,' and told Suzanne, his wife du jour, to do something about it.

"Suzanne, Tiffany is a big girl, why is she sleeping with her brothers in her bed?"

"True George, it doesn't look good."

"You're a woman, will you tell her not to. I worry something might be going on."

Something was going on. They were protecting their sibling from a pedophilic father.

Siding with her husband, Suzanne forbade Tiffany to have her brothers in her bed. What she could not have known, was that she was clearing the way, removing the guards, giving her husband unfettered access to behave badly. Tiffany was determined to minimize her father's access to her body. She and her brothers devised a genius plan: once everyone was settled and before George was transformed into the pestilence that walketh by night, Tiffany would trade rooms with Devonte or Leighton.

Unfortunately neither Devonte nor Leighton could have saved Tiffany one night she was out celebrating a friend's birthday, George turned up amidst the celebration and demanded Tiffany left without delay. He led her to his car and drove off without much fanfare. She knew something was terribly wrong when, instead of taking the familiar way home, he took her to some place she had never even known existed. He stopped the car and began his attack.

She fought.

He overpowered.

His fingers were rammed deep inside her vagina as he ejaculated. I had seen George ejaculate when I was eight years old, only I was too young to know what it was; it was all just white stuff, foam coming from his penis. Tiffany thought about telling Suzanne, then she thought about her grave marked by George's urine. Like a dog marking its territory, George had pissed on the precise spot that was to become Tiffany's eternal home should she be stupid enough to out him, to tell, to seek refuge. Besides, she thought, her relationship with her stepmother was so badly deteriorated that Suzanne would have just thought her stepdaughter a troublemaker, an ingrate who couldn't summon the decency to be thankful to her father for rescuing her from the ills of Jamaica. Nonetheless Tiffany wanted to tell Suzanne her reasons for not wanting to be home alone with her dad; she wanted to tell her why she was always in a bad mood; Tiffany wanted to tell her stepmother why, only with her brothers in her bed did she feel safe enough to sleep.

⟞

The years past, none free of fondling and fending, none ever free of her father's fancy. Tiffany was relieved when Suzanne and George took a trip to Florida. It meant a daughter could be a daughter without her father constantly attacking. She had been sent to stay with Suzanne's sister Michelle.

"It was so refreshing to be at Aunty Michelle's. I was free, you know what I mean?"

I knew what she meant.

Tiffany was free. She no longer had to do everything possible to ensure she was never alone with her father. She no longer had to wait till just before bedtime before going home. She no longer had to have her brothers stand guard in her bed, sleeping only when sandwiched between them. She was free. That freedom came to an end with the return of her father and Suzanne.

But Tiffany preferred nights uninterrupted so she defied orders to return home. She stayed with Michelle until she could no longer ignore the demands for her return.

"I couldn't go back though, you know what I mean. I just had to tell."

Tiffany shared the horrors of her reality with Michelle who shared with her sister Suzanne. The 'you know what' hit the proverbial ceiling and before long, everyone knew of Tiffany's tale. Suzanne took Khadija, the daughter she shared with George and moved clear across the Atlantic to America. Hoping nothing had yet happened to Khadija, Suzanne took a preemptive step. She had to get Khadija as far away as possible from her husband, Khadija's own father.

Tiffany can barely remember the circumstances of her return to George's house, but found that even the threat of jail and the shame of exposure did not convert her father.

"I remember just getting out of the shower one evening and I always made it a point to make sure I had my shorts on."

Tiffany was wearing her shorts, long baggy shorts, when George struck. He fought to pull it off. She was determined to keep it on. The shorts settled at her knees. Not down, but not up either. Despite the struggle, he managed to ram his finger in her vagina. He ejaculated.

"I just remembered looking down and there was all that semen coming out of his penis. I felt so disgusted, so dirty. I just wanted to die."

The next day Tiffany left, unsure of her destination. She spent months sleeping on the couches of do-gooders.

Then age 17, Tiffany fell pregnant. Wanting some semblance of stability and security for her unborn child,
Tiffany returned to the only certainty she knew, she
returned to her father's house. George had by then, moved
Princess into the bed he had shared with Suzanne. Princess
was a relatively close kin to the Montgomerys, with whom
George had had two young children. Tiffany was back in
the house, with her cousin, barely older than herself, as
her new stepmother.

"I found myself pregnant and scared. I had nowhere to go.
But at least I figured I was old enough AND I was seven and a
half months pregnant. He wouldn't try anything."

She was wrong. Not wanting to risk being penetrated
by her father, she had taken the precaution to switch rooms
with her brother Leighton; Devonte had long severed ties with
his father, and found the courage to legally change his name,
distancing himself from the monster he inherited as a father.
Devonte had even been brave enough to thank his father for
teaching him what kind of man *not* to be.

One night after a very pregnant Tiffany had returned to
George's house, she made sure Leighton slept in her bed, while
she slept in his. It would have been silly to alert George; that
would have foiled the plan; that would have added no layers of
protection. Unaware of the switch, George entered Tiffany's
room. Completely naked and fully erect, he didn't even bother
sneaking into the room. There was no need; Khadija with
whom Tiffany shared a bunk bed, was thousand of miles out
of her father's reach. Like I said, Khadija's mother wanted to
ensure *her* daughter was properly off a father's radar. America
had seemed a safe, physical distance. She might have been

unable to save her stepdaughter; she was hell-bent on saving her own.

With no need to tip toe, George climbed into Tiffany's bed.

He slithered under the covers.

He hugged the body from behind.

His intended wasn't there.

He had groped and grinded on his son Leighton.

Tiffany had had enough. Her pregnancy was obviously no deterrent; it engendered no sympathy, it installed no boundaries.

With that realization, she was ready to trade the certainty of a roof for the freedom of the unknown, the sanctity of the streets. George was determined his daughter, pregnant or not, was to remain in his house. If she *was* in the house, she couldn't go to the police as she'd threatened. George wanted to ensure his freedom; he was determined to stay out of the prison to which he subjected his daughter.

"Yuh naw leave out of dis house a bloodclawt."

"You're a sick fuck and you can't stop me," Tiffany bellowed from her soul.

George grabbed his machete and slapped it on the countertops and on the kitchen cupboards, in a way meant to relay his seriousness.

"Mi say yuh not coming out here."

"Try and stop me you sick fuck."

"Put one more foot toward di door and watch me chop up yuh bloodclawt."

Tiffany took the step.

George proved he meant what he said. He raised the machete in earnestness and only stepped back when his cousin-concubine stepped between father and daughter.

"George, what the fuck you doing?" Princess screamed. "It's your daughter, she's pregnant."

"Mek she know I'm serious Princess. Mi will kill har bloodclawt."

Tiffany took advantage of the conversation between George and Princess and headed toward the front door. George went in pursuit. He grabbed at his daughter's foot as she ascended the stairs toward the door to freedom. She kicked in defense. Fully enraged, he pursued as a lion on the brink of starvation pursuing a wounded hyena. He wanted Tiffany, her body, her obedience and her silence.

"Get away from me you fucking pedophile!" Tiffany shouted.

With those words, George retreated. His rage was suddenly gone and he sat, defeated, deflated, forced to hear what he was, a "fucking pedophile."

Though Tiffany has since had no contact with her father, she still suffers. She remains haunted by her father. She remains haunted by the possibility her father's "sickness" might just be hereditary. She worries for her son. She fears for her daughter. She, without wanting to, lashes out at her fiancé who loves her dearly. He wants to know why she only sleeps with her back towards him. She tells him simply:

"I don't want your breath on me; I don't want you in my face."

✝ ✝ ✝

*And she fled into the wilderness, where she hath
a place of God, that they should feed her there a
thousand two hundred [and] threescore days.*

—Revelations 12:6

went so far off track. I had started telling you about running from Norburt's house, wasn't I? Well, having just fled Norburt's, I boarded the B47 heading toward the 90s. I didn't have money for the bus fare but I earned the pity of the bus driver who motioned me to sit. I didn't have clothes. I didn't have a plan. I didn't have trust or faith. I had nothing, and with nothing but brokenness, I went to my good Uncle Junior, who might have surmised what happened but didn't ask questions. Or he might have gotten a call from Winsome warning him to watch out for me. Who knew, who cared? My good Uncle Junior just fed his 'Baby Girl.' A few days later he retrieved my things from Norburt's and Rutland Road became my new home. And though there might have been loiterers and gunshots, I felt safe, protected. I could easily tell the enemy, the unsavory. Actually, it was easy to avoid the unsavory because everyone knew who they were, they weren't predators disguised as uncles. Or were they?

I appreciated my good Uncle Junior, and loved him for protecting me. He had long been separated form Beuhla and had rented an apartment steps from Beuhla's. But the truth be known I felt like an inconvenience, a burden; he had, after all, ceded his comfort of his bedroom so I could have some semblance of peace. I decided it was time to give my good uncle back his freedom and comfort; it was time to try Mumfort Taylor. He was my father after all. I followed Mumfort's directions and took the train then the bus to his house on Springfield Boulevard in the Cambria Heights section of Queens. There was no time for small talk, where would I have begun? I simply reminded him I needed a place to stay for a while. Not why, just that I did. I could see that the woman standing alongside Mumfort was none too pleased and had obviously objected but he'd never done anything for me, besides hoisting my dress. He owed me that much, didn't he?

Olga, the woman at Mumfort's side, was an unfortunate looking woman with a face of a million worries. I had known she had one of those telling names, but had hoped her name betrayed her beauty. I had hoped that upon meeting her I'd see that her looks proved otherwise. They didn't. She was singularly unattractive. It could have been her inability to bear children. It could have just been her pedigree. Her lips sagged, almost to stray from the rest of her face, I imagined from years of nagging. They hung low enough to touch her neck without much effort. She was short, and the oversized ankle-length clothes she wore only made her look shorter. I thought she was Mumfort's mother until he said, "this is your Aunt Olga."

'She might be your wife but she's no relative of mine,' I thought. We don't have ugly people in our family. We might have predators and evildoers, but at least they were good-looking, easy on the eyes. We had grown up expecting ugly things from ugly people and good things from good-looking people. Wasn't it easier to hide behind a pretty façade than a foreboding one? And, do you remember being scared of the pretty next door or the ugly down the road? Anyway, "could she be any uglier?" I thought, praying it was indeed a thought and that I hadn't said it out loud.

Indeed Mumfort's wife was not at all what I expected. 'How did she, so ugly get to foreign?' If my mother, the 'looker' was the love of Mumfort's life, why would he have settled for a gnome with oversized glassed that made her eyes look like they belonged on tarsier? And I had thought if I were her hair, I would just as hurriedly recede from a forehead the size of a breadfruit, run in flight from such a face.

Mumfort reiterated to his wife that I needed a place to stay for a while. The gnome protested just to register her protest. She knew it was futile but had to let Mumfort know she did not appreciate his bastard child, born to an attempted home wrecker, being in her house. All the same, Mumfort said I could stay for a while and with that asked Olga to show me to my holding area.

⸻◦⸻

It was a modest house, typical of Jamaicans—or anyone really—who were surprised they had risen above their circumstances to amass worldly treasures. It was crammed with furniture, cloaked, and I imagine suffocating, in plastic armor. It was obviously furniture collected throughout the years. Even the decades-old carpet was covered in plastic. If ever there was really an ice palace Mumfort's house was its plastic rival.

Deer carcasses were the only sign of life. Mumfort pleasured himself by shooting deer and proudly displayed their heads on the walls, their feet turned into lamp bases and their skins turned into lampshades.

The rooms were dark, heavy drapes ensured the sunlight kept its place, outside. The house wasn't small, but it wasn't large: two bedrooms on the first floor, three on the second floor. It might have been enough for the barren couple, but the grown son of one of Mumfort's childhood friends occupied one bedroom on the first floor; Mumfort and Olga the second.

Most of the second floor was designated to Mumfort's niece Marjorie, her husband and child. A third upstairs bedroom belonged to Norma, Olga's sister, who, though she was a live-in maid, had her dedicated room at Mumfort's. Olga had an old sofa bed brought up from the basement. It smelled old, musty, moldy and uninviting. If the smell wasn't repelling enough, protruding innersprings made damn sure comfort was banished. That became my bedroom, strictly assigned to easing night into day. It and all its discomforts were to remind me that my being at Mumfort's was to be a temporary arrangement; any illusion of ease might have enticed me to want to stay.

The reclaimed sofa bed was put in Norma's room, and that's where I'd be spending my time. I'd be sleeping on the sofa on which Mumfort and Olga's 100-pound German Shepherd Brutus had slept until it became to displeasing to him. He really was a brute, suited to his name. He was confined to the basement so as not to be a liability to his owners. He'd jump the fence, climb under the fence, anything to get at passersby or worse, people ringing the doorbell. If the basement was Brutus' domain, the sofa was his throne, until I got there anyway, and the dog's bed was reassigned to me. I was sure that like Olga, Brutus resented me. He'd growl and snarl and grimace to show his displeasure.

I limited the time spent at Mumfort's to nights on the sofa with the poking wires. I'd work, ride the subway, go to the Village; I'd go anywhere until nightfall and I was sure it was just enough time to get back to Mumfort's, go straight upstairs, shower and sleep. That routine would be interrupted only when thirst forced me to the first floor to get a can of soda from Olga's fridge. She had made it a point to show me what I could and couldn't touch; water or Coke was fine, any deviation would be frowned upon or worse met with words that would force her, another devoted child of God, to later ask forgiveness.

I didn't want her things or her rebuke; I didn't want her to talk to me through the hypocritical lips with which she praised her God. I didn't want to breathe her air. But I needed a place to rest my head so my good Uncle Junior didn't have to sacrifice.

One night, I was tired, tired of the springs poking me, tired of imagining I was enveloped in clean spring scents, not the stale smell of dog and dog piss. I was tired of imagining comfort so I traded the stinking sofa for Norma's unoccupied, inviting bed with its comforter and decorative pillows. Olga must have crept in during the night and saw me in her sister's bed. The next morning I was rebuked. I wondered why her sister, a live-in maid who came by every other weekend got the comfortable bed while I was relegated to broken springs in a piss-infused dog bed. I was sure Olga knew I disliked her more than her God would allow *her* to hate me. But she had the handle and I had the blade. She had the power and could leave her brute to roam when she and Mumfort retired to bed, knowing all the damn dog wanted to do was rip me to shreds for taking what was his. One night, Brutus the beast lunged and I dodged. I ran upstairs faster than I had run from an uncle in pursuit. I took my duffle bag (yes, I was living out of a duffle bag, made for easy transportation) and went back to my good Uncle Junior. He might have been inconvenienced but I would not be shredded—at least not by a damn dog. I stayed at my Uncle Junior's even after Beuhla, his 300-plus pound girlfriend from whom he was long separated but obviously still not detached, made sure I knew my place. A registered nurse by trade, one would expect her to possess a certain empathy and compassion. But not Beuhla; she had told me how displeased she was that my uncle was providing me a refuge. Her words cut like a hot knife into butter:

"Don't think you can use T to jump from one uncle's bed to another."

I never understood why she called my uncle T, nonetheless I didn't tell him what Beuhla had said, not because I wanted to shield her, but because I wanted to keep my uncle from going to prison for maiming or killing the whale of a woman.

✝　✝　✝

And Adam said, This [is] now bone of my bones, and flesh of my flesh: she shall be called Woman, because she was taken out of Man. Therefore shall a man leave his father and his mother, And shall cleave unto his wife: And they shall be one flesh.

—Genesis 2:23-24

I wondered how I'd gotten the job as a gal Friday in the shipping department at a major production company—in Manhattan. Me, Julie from Jamaica was working in Manhattan. Even if back in those days it was not prestigious to be housed near the Westside Highway, I was working in the City that never sleeps. That part of town was for the prostitutes and their pimps but hey, I had a job through which my life would change—again! Olivia, another Jamaican at work became my friend. Forget that she was old enough to be my mother, or perhaps it was for that reason that she, a childless woman already living in America for three decades, became my mentor.

She loved classical music and introduced me to it. I thought she was mad or epileptic the way she bobbed her head, sending her Indian bangs flailing, as she pretended to conduct the music blasting on her radio, but I grew to love Bach and Beethoven and Tchaikovsky. I grew to love Olivia. She was the mother I thought I might have picked. I know, presumptuous.

Olivia took me to Lincoln Center and Central Park and The Plaza Hotel, places other than my routine. I was getting to know places I'd never even had the cranial bandwidth to imagine, and probably never would have were it not for her insistence I became comfortable with things and places other than Brooklyn.

And she introduced me to Jerome.

Jerome no-middle-name Washington, had been a high school basketball star. Not particularly tall, but apparently with enough talent and determination to be compared to Spud Webb, the 5'7" NBA phenom, who despite being one of the shortest players in NBA history went on to win a slam dunk contest. Jerome had been quite the superstar and kept all the newspaper clippings to prove. His tales were long, mostly interesting but bordered on boring when they became repetitious.

Jerome was Lee's good son. Lee, born Eunice Mae Johnson, had three sons: Leonard the repeat offender and perpetual inmate; John the severely autistic man-boy who'd hit himself so hard in the head he detached his retina in the right eye; and Jerome, the basketball star on whom all hopes hung. Lee made sure Jerome knew it too, that he was her only pension plan. She encouraged him, and though his basketball heydays were best viewed in a clean rear-view mirror, Jerome knew he was the ticket to transcend the projects they called home. I thought it strange that 'they' called it projects and in Jamaica we called it tenement yard.

Anyway, in relentless pursuit of a business degree from Long Island University, Jerome was aware of Lee's plans for his life and tried never to displease her. And she wasn't easily pleased. In fact, I often thought her the American version of Dee. She was from Georgia, the 'deep' South, and that, I thought, helped reinforce her rigidity. She was nothing short of overbearing.

Lee spoke with a drawl that made it necessary to give her my undivided attention to make sure I knew what she was saying. But I'm getting ahead of myself because I was telling you about Jerome. But since everyone knew chip nuh fly far from the block, the two were inextricable, mother and son.

Jerome was 23, I was 18 but Olivia knew we'd be perfect for each other. He was completing his final classes at LIU while he worked as a clerk at a sporting goods store near Columbus Circle. He was charming, amenable and even tolerable. But most attractive about him was that he wanted to do something with *his* life, and didn't dwell on his failed attempt at the NBA.

I liked that in him that he didn't really dwell on his shortcomings. He relived them, but didn't really dwell on them.

And he wasn't bad looking even if we were just about the same height. He had beautiful, full kissable lips. And despite the bridge that replaced the teeth knocked out by basketball, he was perfect for me. Before we even defined what we had, we didn't want to be apart for more than the compulsory time for work. We dressed alike, yes exactly alike. We did couples' things: movies, dinners, walks, plays. I watched him play basketball on West 4th Street in the Village. I really had absolutely no interest in watching just-missed-their-chance-at-the-NBA grown men battle for street creds, but had to supported my Jerome. I often spent hours gnawing at Nathan's hot dogs and nursing a soda while cheering from the sideline. I wasn't the only girlfriend who sat in support of their loves; there were others, lots of supportive girlfriends, including Bernadine, girlfriend to Jerome's best friend Jason.

Bernadine was barely tolerable. Actually, she was intolerable, abrasive even. She was a transplant from Trinidad and thought her Indian-Afro hybrid made her superior. I'd met her kind before and had the good sense to completely blank her. You know, treat her with the same attention reserved for a persona non grata. Some damn gyal who thought her shit didn't stink. Don't get me wrong, we were cordial, but unlike our boyfriends, we weren't friends nor did we delude ourselves with hope. I was glad when she and Jason married and decided to live the settled, expected married life. It meant our encounters would be, at best, occasional and brief.

The months flew by and Jerome and I had been dating for just over a year, though our living arrangements made love difficult. Not impossible, just difficult.

Jerome, the good son, lived with his mother and brother John in Alphabet City. It was a mutual convenience: Jerome didn't have to pay rent and Lee had a live-in manservant to tend John's needs brought on by his disability.

Lee made no secrets she didn't like me, and might have even hated me. She would feign tolerance when my Uncle Junior and I visited. Lee never visited my good uncle Junior. Actually, did she ever venture out of Alphabet City?

Jerome was mostly uncomfortable with Junior's generosity of freedom to come see me whenever he could peel himself from Lee. Maybe it was the male pride because I couldn't quite understand why my uncle's caring was a bad thing. It wasn't like *I* was welcomed at Lee's. And though she'd rather not have a 'Jamaican girl' in her apartment, she was too selfish to let go of Jerome to get his own place. She needed the help. Apparently we were stuck between Lee's ice-laced tolerance and Junior's too-open welcome. It was often easier to ride the train, any train, from dusk to dawn. Jerome and I rode the F Train, the E

Train, the 1, 2, 4, 5, the R Train. Quasi-homelessness was not what I'd imagined of and for life in America.

Seaforth might have been in Jamaica and not of America but I was ready to go back to my familiar where my bed still remained, where I would not have to ride trains till sun up. The urge to go home might have been brought on by the impending birth of a new decade. The 80s, so unkind to me in so many ways, were coming to a close and something inside me also yearned for change. I wondered how much things might have changed back home, and was happy when I learned that indeed they had. George had been forced to marry his girlfriend Nicole if they were to have conjugal encounters at Pops' house. Lucky for George, Nicole was a citizen of the crown, born and raised in England until her parents repatriated when Nicole was a teenager. The new couple was encouraged to move to London where more opportunities of all sorts abounded. I wasn't necessarily happy for them and the hopes life in England might have held for them, I was happy for my sisters I no longer had to worry might have been left alone in the care of the pedophile we inherited as an uncle.

If I went back home, I wouldn't have to deal with his perpetual attacks. Oin had died. And though I missed the way he would cup his farts in his hand and then put his hand over our noses, at least I wouldn't have to go visit any obeah man professing to help my brother while hurting me. Going back was attractive, even if it meant never being able to reenter America. But what would I care, in certain aspects everyday Jamaica had followed me to America. America, at least the America I knew had lost its luster and the unspoiled memories of my Jamaica had resurfaced.

I finally summoned the courage to share my predicament with Jerome: I loved him but hated riding the trains till sun up. I loved being with him but desperately yearned for my familiar.

"Why don't we go visit?" he asked. "We're both working, why don't we just plan a trip?"

"Well, that's what I needed to talk to you about. You see…"

"We can probably get a couple weeks off…" he interrupted before I clipped his sentence.

"You don't understand, I can go but I couldn't come back with you."

"You don't want to be with me anymore?

"That's not it Jerome, I love you and I want to be with you but…"

"So we'll just go for a couple of weeks."

"Jerome, I couldn't come back, not that I might not want to. I couldn't."

I had to explain, a couple times why I couldn't reenter America, at least not legally. I was an illegal alien. I don't remember Jerome being surprised at my revelation; he was more confused and resolute. His solution left me dumbfounded but pleased.

"I'll marry you so you could stay here with me. I can do that, can't I?"

"I want to," Jerome insisted.

"But what will Lee say?"

"I want you to stay here, Julie."

"I know, I want to…"

"Listen, I'm a grown man, I'm 24 years old and Ma is just gonna have to respect my decisions."

"Jerome, I appreciate it but..."

"This is what we're doing, Julie. I mean, we're both adults, right?"

Jerome was right; we were both adults in the eyes of the law. I was not old enough to drink but I could marry with no one's permission, and on March 14, 1988, I became Mrs. Julie Marie Washington. No fanfare, no flowing white wedding gowns and ring bearer and brides maids and groomsmen and proud parents; just Jerome and I and our required witness at city hall. Civil.

While I told my mother who registered her displeasure I got married at such a young age, neither Jerome nor I had what it took to tell his mother. Jerome, however, definitely developed strength and asked his mother if I could stay with them. Though Lee made it no secret she'd much rather her son fall in love with a good southern girl, she was by some miracle persuaded to let me stay with them for a little bit. There were conditions and stipulations, strings attached. Jerome had to share room with John and I was to stay in Jerome's room. The doors were never to be closed and I was to pay rent and bills and help with the housework. Lee did all the cooking. She enjoyed it and I loved her cooking.

Jerome and Lee argued too regularly for a grown man and his mother who needed him, or at least needed his companionship. I knew I was the source of the contentions but at least they were never directed at me, just about me.

"Why you couldn't find a nice Southern girl Drome?" Yea, she meant Jerome but her Southern drawl prevented her from saying her son's name as it was intended.

"Ma, I'm 24 years old. You gotta stop trying to run my life."

"Well maybe you should take your damn coc'nat girl and leave, this is my house."

"Maybe we'll just do that, but every time we try to leave you start crying Ma."

"I don't give a shit Drome, I can't take no dam Jewmakin in ma house."

"Ma, that's my wife you're talking about Ma."

"Yo what bwah? What did you say bwah? Your what?"

"Yea Ma, that's my wife and you're gonna have to respect her."

"Bwah, you better get the hell out ma house and take your damn coc'nat girl with you...Bwah you did what? You married a mothafuckin Jewmakin? What the fuck Drome? You never would have gotten married without telling me Drome. She turned you 'genz me Drome. I knew it, that's how these fuckin Jewmakins is Drome, day always mothafuckin taking ova Drome."

"Ma, what are you talking about Ma? I didn't tell you because I knew this is how you would act Ma. Ma? Stop crying Ma."

"Dis don't make no damn sense Drome. You never disrespected me like this. In ma own house Drome? In ma own mothafuckin house Drome? No dis ain't go work Drome..."

My husband and I rented a small studio Street in the Hell's Kitchen. Yes, we went to live in Hell's Kitchen where we had to climb over drug addicts and prostitutes—and sometimes their excrements—to enter our building; but it was our very own apartment, free from Lee's tirades.

We loved the freedom of sleeping together as man and wife. I enjoyed sex with him, and him with me. Thoughts of my uncles would only occasionally seep in and ruin our intimacy. We were relieved we no longer had to live with the fear of being found out we were man and wife. We could wear our rings openly and with pride. I was his wife and he was my husband and he didn't care if I wasn't from the South or that I was from Jamaica.

⁓

Lee cooled enough to want to see where her son was living. I couldn't see the value in her visit, wasn't willing to have her contaminate our space; so naturally I objected. Objection sustained. Besides by then, the doctor at St. Luke's Roosevelt Hospital a few blocks from where we lived was baffled I didn't know I was pregnant. I had missed periods before and I'd always had low blood pressure that made me prone to dizzy spells but still should have known something was up when I couldn't keep anything down, or will my eyes to stay awake.

Jerome and I were expecting our first child. We were pleased. We weren't sure how we'd provide health, stability, education, protection, security, self-esteem and a shield from predators, but we loved the life growing inside me.

Everything else would fall into place. Six months into my pregnancy with a baby girl, I got news that my green card was ready for pick up at the US Embassy in New Kingston, Jamaica. Synergy. I had a husband and a new apartment, even if it was in Hell's Kitchen. There was a new baby girl growing inside me and I *knew* to whom she belonged and would not even have to contemplate dislodging her from my womb. A new residence status was in sight, and with that came a chance to see my familiar *and* pick up my green card, my adjustment of status.

They had failed to tell me it wasn't a matter of formality where I'd walk into the Embassy an illegal alien and out a Resident Alien of the United States of America. Instead weeks turned into to months and pregnancy into baby girl Jennifer Taylor Washington, born October 20, 1989, in the former TB Ward at Princess Margaret Hospital. The maternity ward was still in disrepair, victim of Hurricane Gilbert. At least I had my mother to make me chicken soup after my daughter's arrival. I needed that chicken soup to soothe my innards. And I swore it even eased the barbarism of natural childbirth and having to walk from the 'birthing bed' back to my own after giving birth with not so much as an aspirin. In fact, the attending nurse was the most brutish person I had ever encountered, worse than Hyacinth back when I was 15. The brute for a nurse yelled and barked at women trying to push out their bastards, telling them to shut up because they weren't crying when they were making the babies so they most definitely shouldn't be crying at their current predicaments. She should have been the greeter at hell's gate, not the first thing new babies were subjected to upon their arrival. But then I thought if the Bible was right and we were all born in sin and shaped in inequities, then that was God's idea of a warm welcome.

Jerome missed his daughter's birth by a few days, but came to see her as soon as humanly possibly. He was all too proud to have brought exactly what I had ordered: stroller, bassinet, clothes, pacifiers—and the like. He refused to stop kissing her and stared at her enough to make her poop green, if you believed old folks who warned against such ills; wasn't good for a newborn to be the recipient of such unceasing stares.

My attorney back in America had exhausted appeals and was nearing the end of what he could do for me when he had filed a special petition, a Humanitarian Parole, with the Department of Justice. It was granted, finally, and two weeks after Jennifer's birth, she, Jerome and I left for New York: Jerome and Jennifer United States citizens, me a legal Resident Alien.

Jerome had given up on Hell's Kitchen and returned to Lee's at her insistence as she was convinced I would remain in Jamaica where I belonged. She couldn't understand why her son would waste *his* time and *our* money visiting me there while the lawyer fought for my return. Lee understood less why he would fly to the 'tird world country' a second time to see his first-born. It was hard for me to return to Lee's but had to again endure her special brand of bile. The addition of her first grandchild did little to ease the tension. How could it have when she only ever referred to my daughter as "coc'nat baby?"

I found work fast. It was so much easier as a Resident Alien. I no longer had to worry because I was a bona fide, legal permanent resident of the United States of America and no longer had to dodge requests for my social security card or other 'acceptable' documents that said I could legally work in the US. I had considered myself so unlucky, that not even a year after I'd arrived in New York, President Ronald Reagan signed the Immigration Reform & Control Act into law on November 6, 1986. IRCA made it illegal for employers to knowingly hire or recruit unauthorized immigrants. In other words, employers had to "attest to their employees immigration status." IRCA

was no longer my concern though, and within weeks of returning from Jamaica, I became a receptionist at one of America's
Big Six accounting firms. I was working, legally, in a respectable part of town—midtown Manhattan.

A couple months later Jerome and I moved our daughter to
the Fairview Apartments near Flushing Meadow Park, home of
the US Tennis Open. It was a great big apartment, with a dedicated uniformed doorman. Guests had to be announced. We
didn't have to hopscotch over druggies and prostitutes to gain
entrance. Life was good. And to make it better, we arranged
for Mawma to come up from Jamaica to babysit Jennifer. I
didn't trust babysitters. Soon after, my mother would join us,
so Mawma could go to regular day school. Life was good; it
might not have been perfect but it was getting closer to the
America I'd grown up envisioning, encouraged of course by
television.

✣ ✣ ✣

Let the sighing of the prisoner come before thee; According to the greatness of thy power preserve thou those that are appointed to die.

—Psalms 79:11

had been enjoying the quiet of the evening when the phone rang. It was a collect call from Jerome's prison bird brother Leonard. It was Leonard who intimated that something might have been wrong in my marriage, being the first to clue me in that his brother wasn't wholly happy.

"Julie, it's Leonard." I wanted to say I know you dumb motherfucker, I accepted the collect call, but instead opted for a more polite, even if an altogether insincere greeting.

"Hi Leonard, Jerome is not home," I said with enough frustration I was sure he could have felt it. I had never particularly cared for Leonard, though I'd never met him. The stories about him made him less than endearing I thought, and I was sure Lee had fed her caged son enough information to make him despise me. Hatred was a two-way street where Leonard Washington was concerned.

"Well I really wanted to talk to you actually."

"Me? How are you anyway?" I asked, already knowing how he was—stripped of his freedom after the umpteenth time being caught selling massive amounts of drugs. Lee had apparently taken it hard when her son was again sent away. I had suspected her disappointment was not so much in the fact that Leonard would be confined, but more that she would no longer be beneficiary of his spoils; no more mink coat, no more brand new furniture and wall-to-wall carpeting for her government-assisted apartment.

"I came with Jerome to see you [at Riker's] but I didn't have my ID so I had to wait outside…"

"Yea, yea. That's all good. I ain't got time for chit chat."

I wanted to say, 'stop your nonsense Leonard, you have all the time in the world,' but I tried not to stoop to him in his situation.

"Excuse me?"

"You heard me. I want you to get your fucking Jamaican family out of my brother's house."

"What you talking about Leonard? I pay half the rent moth-erfucker, so it's *our* house!" I shouted with enough gusto for the wardens to hear hoping they would register how much their prisoner was bothering me, a free, law-abiding woman, hoping they would grab the phone from him in protest and leave me to my relaxing.

"Whatever, you can't just move your entire family in on my brother."

"Yow, you locked-up motherfucker, I do what the fuck I want when I want. Who are you to tell me what to do? Fuck you Leonard, but you've probably gotten used to being fucked in the ass by your prison pals. Fuck you all the same! Tell me Leonard, do you moan like a little bitch when you're being rammed? Wait, you must do, you keep going back to prison!"

"Just wait till I get out," he said obviously suppressing the urge to shout. Shouting would have alerted the guards that one of their inmates was engaged in behavior unbecoming, well, a prisoner.

"Yea, what you gonna do motherfucker? I'm here waiting if you EVER get out. We ain't going nowhere Leonard mother-fucking Washington!" I could shout without restrictions.

"Listen you little...."

Leonard's over-the-phone beratement was too much. And wait, I had the power unlike when I was trapped under the body of whomever. There I was, accepting a collect call for which I had to pay, for a fucking ward of the state to scold me. The insult had been too much and I did they only thing I could. I slammed the phone its cradle.

✝ ✝ ✝

*Thou shalt not bow down thyself to them,
nor serve them: For I the Lord thy God [am]
a jealous God, visiting the iniquity of the
fathers upon the children unto the third and
fourth [generation] of them that hate me.*

—Exodus 20:5

Dee had quickly found work as a live-in maid. Mawma continued attending Forest Hills High School and was no longer obligated to watch my Jennifer; Dee was paying us rent to board my sister Jerome and I had uprooted from Jamaica to be of service to us. My mother had bought my sister's dignity. My family was funny like that; we didn't like people taking the piss, especially incarcerated outsiders. We always banded together to fend of attacks from strangers; no one of the outside was given permission to abuse, berate or in any way cause discomfort. We had family for that.

Lucky for us—Jerome and I, that is, we found a babysitter in our building. Talk about convenience. And at least she was female and she seemed trustworthy. She was watching other babies, and they all seemed adjusted.

Jennifer wasn't a particularly fussy baby. She was quite pleasant, prone to smiles and well, happy. So when she wouldn't stop crying when I picked her up from the sitter's one evening, I took my daughter straight to the emergency room, something must have been wrong.

Something was wrong. The doctor asked me to wait with my daughter on my lap while he went in an adjoining room. He must have wanted me to hear the conversation because he did nothing to lower his voice or talk in codes.

"My name is Greenbaum. I have to report my findings. Yes, I'll wait."

'Report his findings? What findings? What was he talking about.' I thought about taking my daughter and…

"Yes, the child has signs of molestation around her vaginal area. The skin is bruised and peeling…"

'Signs of WHAT?'

"No it's not a diaper rash. It's consistent with abrasion."

'WHAT!' I thought with enough confusion to make my head again threaten explosion.

"No, I don't think it was the mother, she is here with the child now."

'You don't think I did WHAT?'

The doctor reentered the room with a security officer. They took Jennifer and I to another room. We waited an eternity, under the watchful eye of the officer, for a representative for the New York's Office of Family of Children & Family Services. She eventually showed up with her clipboard and a million questions. She was as caustic as I was confused. What the hell was OCFS doing talking to me, Julie, who loves my child. I wasn't a welfare recipient or one of those people who'd hurt their child. I wondered if they were going to take my Jennifer? I'd seen them yank helpless children from the clutches of desperate mothers. I held Jennifer till I was sure her circulation was permanently affected. Hours passed, a million questions asked and answered, before the caustic woman told me I could take my daughter with me but that I *had* to be there the following morning when a caseworker would visit my home.

'WHAT?'

Her parting words echoed so loudly I thought I had to once again hold my head under cold water. "Make sure you don't try to leave the country."

The caustic woman and another caseworker were at my apartment before I had enough time to properly wake up. I could see why each had become a caseworker; a job suited to folks with feigned compassion and misdirected suspicions I thought. There they were at my door, as overweight as they were overzealous, I thought. Anyway, I had barely slept the night before, spending much of the night staring at Jennifer through the bars on her crib. She slept; I stared. I wondered who and why and how and when and why. I wondered how that could have happened in the presence of such vigilance. I had barely fallen asleep when she awoke. I changed her, fed her, loved her, and vowed to protect her in perpetuity.

The bang at the door startled. I wondered why the doorman hadn't announced their arrival. They were after all visitors who needed permission to enter.

"Good morning Mrs. Washington."

"Good morning."

"We're am going to take a look around."

"Why?"

"It's protocol. We are here to make sure this is a safe environment for your daughter."

"Why wouldn't it be?"

They must not have heard me because the caustic woman took her clipboard and went from room to room, jotting notes and shaking her head knowingly. I didn't understand why she needed to examine the kitchen and the balcony and places a baby had no business being. The other unpleasant woman tackled the bedrooms.

"Where is your husband?"

"He's at work."

"Is he often here?"

"He *lives* here," I said with such sarcasm it sounded more like a question than a response.

"You'll have to surrender your passport."

"Why do you need my passport?"

"I'm most definitely not giving you my passport," I said, wondering if these people had any idea how hard it was for me to get the US officials to validate my passport with their stamp. Hell, I had had to stuff a pillow under my shirt, simulating pregnancy, so they wouldn't question why I had been granted Humanitarian Parole after all. That parole was based on my carrying the seed an American citizen in my womb. I was sure that if they knew I had given birth without incident, they might have rescinded the offer. See, my attorney had made sure they knew mine was an at-risk pregnancy for which I needed Grade A medical care, the kind unavailable in Seaforth District, St. Thomas, Jamaica.

"Ma'am, it's protocol. We have to make sure you don't try to leave the country until the investigation is concluded."

"And what are you investigating?"

"Mrs. Washington, your daughter was brought to the ER with signs of molestation. It is our responsibility to investigate."

"By all means, don't you think I want to know what happened to my child?"

"Good we are on the same page."

"I'm the one who took her to the hospital, remember?"

"We're going to need to talk to everyone who lives here and who has access to your daughter, and please, do not leave the country in the meantime."

OCFS, that agency tasked with the welfare of children and families, was satisfied none of us in the household molested my daughter. We were absolved of any wrongdoing. I asked why OCFS or the police had done nothing to or about the old convenient babysitter. Though I wasn't satisfied with their "insufficient evidence" retort, life went on. I took Jennifer to a new babysitter near my place of legal employment. It was hardly convenient enduring the train ride from Queens to Manhattan with a child in stroller in tow. But it was a small price to pay for more peace of mind. The new sitter had come highly recommended and with glowing references, traits that trumped convenience. I developed a new obsession though: checking my daughter's diapers, almost incessantly.

～§～

It was the dead of winter 1990. The trees had long shed their leaves. Snow, dirty snow replaced grass. It was cold. It was a cold made worse navigating snow mounds with a stroller. Jennifer and I had finally made it home, hungry for the warmth of a house. I pushed her stroller inside, closed the door behind me and took off my coat. Something was amiss but I'd have to free Jennifer from her snowsuit before I could even bother to determine what was not 'quite right.' It was far too warm inside to leave my baby so insulated.

"We've been robbed!"

I ran from room to room to assess the damage all the while thinking how long the reprobates were in our apartment. Everything was gone: My bed, tables, chairs, sofas, television, etc, you know, all the comforts that said the apartment was occupied, lived in. Everything was gone. Well, almost everything. Jennifer's crib remained the sole item in the bedroom Jerome and I shared; just the crib and the chest with her clothes still sitting in our closet. Most of my clothes were gone too. I was thankful a few sweaters remained on the top shelf.

No, we weren't robbed. Jerome had moved while I was at work. He had moved and had not extended an invitation for his wife and child to join him. And apparently he was in quite the hurry to get away. Why else would he take *my* clothes? He must have not had time to separate his from mine. Mawma got home and had had the same reaction I did though her shock might have been lessened somewhat. Her bed still remained. She and I moved her twin-sized bed into the room with Jennifer's crib. We sat on the living room floor like squatters and ate the fried rice and chicken wings we had ordered from the Chinese restaurant. We cried. We conjectured. We resolved. The apartment was far too big, and too expensive for us, even with our mother's salary. We had to make sensible, if altogether rushed plans. We prioritized, and other than Dee, Mawma and I nobody knew what had happened, that my husband had abandoned his wife and child without so much as "I'm really not happy, this is really not working." He had said none of the clichéd crap spouses tell each other when one stopped loving the other.

We found a tiny railroad apartment on Manhattan's Upper Eastside, 85th Street just off Third Avenue, to be exact. It was clean, almost affordable, and mine. We didn't have much to move from Queens to Manhattan, and settled quickly. Mawma had left Forest Hills High School to work at McDonalds to make up the difference in rent. Dee, Mawma and I pooled our pennies so we could live from paycheck to paycheck. Life wasn't good; it was life, what we had been assigned.

Winter had turned to spring and spring to summer. My sister, mother and I, worked and took Jennifer to the park. Mawma prepared for her GED. My boss decided to send me to its offices on the 97th floor of 1 World Trade Center. The move was good. It was a promotion to pool secretary/relief receptionist but I had been used to working in Midtown, just steps from Times Square. I had to reorient and get used to Downtown, just like I had to get used to working so high in the sky. It was bad enough having to endure the whistle of the elevator shooting to 97th floor, and when it jerked to a stop, my heart would try to leap out of my chest.

I wasn't particularly fond of heights; actually, I hated heights. In fact, as upwardly mobile as I fancied myself, I'd been invited, more than once to the world-renowned Windows of the World restaurant, housed in the North Tower but each time I had declined, preferring the comfort and predictability of Sbarros on the ground floor. Yes, I had, on several occasions, declined to dine where the bosses dined. But it was good; the ground floor didn't shake and sway. It was stable, not wobbly on its quest to reach the sky. The ground floor was predictable. Predictability! I had grown rather fond of predictability. Go to work, do secretarial stuff, go to lunch, relieve the receptionist so she could go to lunch, go back to secretarial stuff, go home to Jennifer.

Almost as much as I loved predictability, I hated laziness, and almost got myself fired when a senior manager exhibited signs of utter inexcusable laziness. On one of my relief duties, Matthew Archer had had the audacity to call the switchboard—from his office mere yards away—to ask if he had messages. It was not enough that everyone in the universe decided to call the switchboard—at the same time. No, I had a lazy senior manager calling to ask if he had messages. My response was simple, really.

"If you want to know if you have messages, why don't you get off your ass and come check?"

I'd hardly put the receiver in the cradle when this giant of a man towered over me. I grabbed my bag ready to walk out before the words 'you're fired' could have been said. But those words never came; the ones that did come shocked the you-know-what out of me. The nearly 7-foot blond, green-eyed giant with the strange accent, said simply, "That was a good one," and went back to his office. Then he came back with a note that read "would you go to the movies with me?"

"Surely this is a trick," I wrote back. Yes, we were passing notes.

"No, I'm dead serious."

"If I say no will I be fired?"

"No, but it would be better if you said yes."

"Yes."

✠ ✠ ✠

*I say therefore unto the unmarried and
widows, it is good for them if they abide as I.
But if they cannot contain, let them marry:
for it is better to marry than to burn. And
unto the married I command, [yet] not I, but
the Lord, Let not the wife depart from [her]
husband: But and if she depart, let her remain
unmarried, or be reconciled to [her] husband:
And let not the husband put away his wife.*

—1 Corinthians 7:8-11

Matthew was meek for a giant, and fast became my boyfriend. I was amenable to a man in my life; that helped ease the unpleasantness of Jerome. That unpleasantness! Matthew was a genius who had worked in Paris, in his native Australia, in New York. He was a success in business. But there was a certain social awkwardness to him. Some might have even called him a nerd, a condition he blamed on his family, all medically inclined: Dr. McMillan Archer, father; Dr. Dorothy Archer, mother; Dr. Roland Archer, brother; Dr. Destin Archer, brother; Dr. Christine Archer, sister-in-law; Dr. Lydia Archer, niece. His father would even go on to be knighted for his work in the studies of infectious diseases, and these days, he is Sir Dr. McMillan Archer. All the medical stuff made Matthew queasy though. He literally fainted at the sight of blood or a needle, and the mere mention of anything medical was enough to make him heave a good heave.

Matthew and I had a great relationship. It was not without its share of questions and quips. Spike Lee's *Jungle Fever* was fresh on everyone's mind and people wanted to know what it was like being in an inter-racial relationship. That was, people who were polite enough to ask, unlike the Muslim 'brothers' in black suits, white shirts and bowties. They who would mimic a throat cutting gesture whenever Matthew and I walked past them. We often had to endure the people who took glee in shouting JUNGLE FEVER! Neither he nor I cared enough to stop loving each other. And he loved Jennifer. Matthew reconstituted *my* family, and often endured the ridicule and finger pointing when he, a massive white man, took Jennifer, a little black girl, to the park without me there for people to make the connection. And he always put her on his shoulders; maybe because he was so tall hunching to push a stroller was just too ridiculous. Whatever, they were inseparable—she was his daughter and he was her dad. He moved us from the tiny railroad apartment to a bigger, brighter apartment in Kew Gardens, Queens. I had suspected he was in a hurry to move us, not because the apartment was that unpleasant, but because we lived on the third floor of a walk up and our downstairs neighbor often yelled racial slurs meant to hasten our departure.

"This is America. We can't have niggas living on top of good white people. Get out monkeys." We got out, not because the crazy white man told us to, but because Matthew was far too big to live with us in what was at best a dedicated closet in a Park Avenue apartment. Our address might have said Upper Eastside but the apartment said 'keep trying to move on up.'

Just two years into the 1990s and things were finally looking up, so to speak: I had a job, having been promoted again I no longer had to relieve the receptionist, minimizing the risk of being fired. That promotion boosted my confidence, and even inspired real aspiration. I later interviewed at a completely new company, and was surprised when I got the job as an administrative assistant at graphics/typesetting firm on Park Avenue South. And, I had a man I loved and who loved my daughter without conditions. I had a man more determined I did something with my own life. He quite literally drove me to St. John's University and made me complete—and submit—an application for admittance. To my surprise, I was accepted. I was a college freshman at age 24; when most kids were looking to graduate and enter the workforce I'd just begun university.

It was just what I needed, when I needed it. What is it they say about timing? I had started a new job, registered for my freshman classes and had enrolled in driving school at Matthew's insistence. He had insisted on a lot of things, things meant for my betterment: 'J', his nickname for me, "you've got to get a college education if you want to compete"; "J, you've got to learn how to drive if you want to reduce your reliance on men"; "J, you've got to let go of the past if you want to succeed in the future"; "J, you've got to find it in yourself to forgive Mumfort and give him a chance to get to know you, I mean to know you is to love you." And so I thought if Matt was right about college and driving, he couldn't be far wrong about Mumfort. I called Mumfort and as you can imagine, the conversation was as expected: awkward, clumsy, father and daughter tripping over words. I told 'my father' I had enrolled in university. I told him I was learning to drive. He offered to help with both.

"Let me know what your expenses are," he said in the most uninspired, unenthused monotone. He sounded more like he was submitting to regrets rather than to the delights of a father's will to help a daughter.

"I will, and thank you."

"I know I haven't always been there but I want you to know I will do everything to help with your education."

"Thank you, I'm determined to make better."

"Tell you what, give me your address, I will come by around 11 on Saturday to take you driving."

Call me gullible; call me optimistic but I was excited, eager for Mumfort to teach me to drive, to teach me anything. I got dressed for learning to drive. I had already signed up with a professional driving instructor, but I relished the idea of Mumfort's tutelage. It was a most palpable anticipation that grew more pronounced as 11 o'clock approached. Anticipation mixed with dread: what was I to say to a virtual stranger who is supposed to be my father? I stood by the bedroom window that afforded the best view of the street. I wanted to see Mumfort arrive and park so I could dash straight out.

Eleven turned to noon and before I knew it was 3pm and I still had my face peeled to the window. I would be lying if I say I wasn't hurt Mumfort didn't show up, or that he hadn't even bothered to call. It would be a bigger lie to say I didn't hate myself for being hurt, worse, for allowing Mumfort's promise to once again engender an emotion or trigger any sort of reaction, voluntary or involuntary. I know, what was I thinking? It was the same Mumfort, who in 1978 had promised to come back for me. Nearly two decades later I had again fallen for his promises. When would I learn a promise is really of comfort to only a fool?

A year of so later I had finally mustered the courage to call Mumfort again, partly at Matt's insistence. His number was disconnected, not changed to a new number, disconnected.

I called the boiler room at Rockefeller Center where he had worked in some capacity or other.

"Mumfort retired dear."

"I asked for Mumfort Taylor, are you sure?"

"Yes dear, Mumfort retired a few months ago and moved to North Carolina."

"Thank you."

I had to hear it from a boiler room clerk that the man who had announced he was my father had retired and moved out of state? Yes, the same guy who made the promises was gone for good, he and his insipid wife.

Matt consoled me, or at least he tried. He assured me that Mumfort was really the one missing out. He held me as I cried uncontrollably. He said he was sorry for insisting I gave Mumfort another try. Matt later confessed it had been one of the saddest things he'd seen, me with face glued to the window, not wanting to miss a father's arrival, only to leave, defeated by the knowledge that he'd never show.

⚬

University was a refuge, and by the fall of 1994, Matt insisted I studied full-time. I was free to quit my job and make the study of journalism my priority, well second only to mothering my Jennifer and loving Matt. Then, barely a month into the new semester, Matt was transferred to his native Australia. There was no dilemma; we were all going to Australia. Matt, Jennifer and I were to move to Sydney, Australia. It was an easy decision, but a hard flight. Matt had gone ahead to prepare, leaving me to finish the semester and to surrender the Kew Gardens apartment.

It would have been hard for seasoned adult travels, it was damn near impossible for an amateur with a five year-old child, no matter how well behaved she might have been. We endured the cross-country trek from New York's JFK to LA, and wasn't sure we would outlast the Los Angeles to Sydney leg—it was long. We did, we were determined and resilient.

Sydney wasn't at all what I expected. It was Boxing Day (day after Christmas) and I had just learned they were really backwards in Australia; December was the peak of the summer. Sweet. We had just traded snow for sun and surf, and for Dorothy's infamous Boxing Day party.

✝   ✝   ✝

My brethren, have not the faith of our Lord Jesus Christ of glory, with respect of persons. For if there come unto your assembly a man with a gold ring, in goodly apparel, and there come in also a poor man in vile raiment; And ye have respect to him that weareth the gay clothing, and say unto him, sit thou here in a good place; and say to the poor, stand thou there, or sit here under my footstool: Are ye then not partial in yourselves, and are become judges of evil thoughts?

—James 2:2-4

D orothy, or more appropriately, Dr. Archer as she preferred to be called, was unusually short to have such a giant for a son. But she did, she was mother to Roland, Matthew and Destin, in that order. She stood barely five feet and boasted home-dyed blond locks to help hide her advancing age. Dorothy was only just overweight but she dressed well enough to hide her less than ideal weight from inquisitive eyes. She wore a special bra to hide the reality of losing her breasts to cancer, and though she had long retired as a practicing physician, she found it difficult to stop dispensing medical advice. She was all 'doctor' but had lacked industriousness when it came to matters of housekeeping. She was what we would call 'nasty' in Jamaica. She preferred entertaining to cleaning, and a dirty house did not stop her invitations to bridge or tea or dinner. McMillan, Matt's father was himself a noted physician often called on for expert testimony or advice. He and Dorothy lived well. Their house sat in one of the most desirable areas of Vaucluse, arguably one of the most affluent areas of Sydney's Eastern Suburbs. The house was grand and boasted an enviable view of the

Sydney Harbour, including the famed Sydney Harbour Bridge. It was unlike anything I'd seen—ever!

Jennifer and I arrived in the midst of Dorothy's party. We were literally the only two black faces among the sea of white, funny sounding people. They were welcoming and friendly but frankly we were exhausted, having just endured a 14-hour non-stop flight from LA to Australia. That didn't include the NY to LA portion. We watched a bit of the boat race, partly because I'd never seen such a collection of boats, yachts and mega yachts, partly because I was trying desperately not to be rude.

Perhaps exhausted, perhaps intimidated, perhaps over-whelmed, I excused myself and slept for the next 10 hours, and when we finally woke up it was to quiet: no boats, no music, no sea of strangers.

Dorothy had done her best to make us feel welcome. She had prepared a room for Jennifer, complete with a mobile she made by hand, hand-painted pictures meant to make her feel at home and enough toys to keep her mind off her jetlag. Matt and I had another room overlooking the Sydney Harbor. Not too shabby. Parsley Bay was just across the street, and made for quick escape when getting to know Dorothy and McMillan became overwhelming.

Two days after arriving in Sydney, I called Lee, Jerome's mother back in the States, to give her our updated address and phone number, in hopes she would relay the information to her son with whom we had had no contact since he moved out. We had no address, no phone number, no contact, and though I always called his mother to ensure they, mother and son, a conduit to Jennifer, they never used it. *They* never called or wrote. *They* never bothered.

In fact, the only information Lee did convey to her son was that I had "kidnapped" Jennifer and moved to Australia. I suspected her saying I kidnapped Jennifer was meant to show her son how horrible a human being I was; I was certain that her strategy was meant to spur no other reaction, like that of care or longing or even anger. But though I was not to know till some years later, upon hearing the news, Jerome had apparently suddenly sprouted affection for his daughter, the same affection that caused him to consult the 'authorities' in an attempt to have them order our return to America—and have me prosecuted. I had had no idea I was the subject of an investigation nor could I fathom why I'd be. Fathers who abandon children and shun all attempts at communication were not necessarily beacons of responsibility.

The 'authorities' must have surmised the vindictiveness of a deadbeat father should never have be mistaken for altruistic paternal pursuits. They must have known that Lee had not passed on school reports and school pictures and updated addresses and phone numbers to her son. Not that he might have cared, mind you. We weren't in hiding, weren't hard to find. If he wanted, he could have feigned fatherhood, I thought; I had always made it easy with the unrequited outreach. I had hoped I was creating an avenue to his child, no strings attached, not even a request for child support. All I wanted was for a daughter to know her father, and a father her daughter. But it had finally become obvious that when Jerome left, *he* had cut all ties. He wanted to stay gone. It would soon become apparent that I needed to stop trying so hard.

Not long after we had been in Australia, Jennifer picked up the phone and asked the operator for the whereabouts of her father. Something had to be done. The whole situation was becoming too absurd. See, unfortunately the folks in that part of Australia had scarcely seen black people. Sure they saw Aboriginals on television, but we weren't Aboriginals. We looked different and though we spoke English, it was not with the tongue with which they were familiar. We still said shrimp, they said prawns; we said under shirt, they said singlet; we said cantaloupe, they said rock melon; we said red pepper, they said capsicum, for example.

The adults had filters that mostly kept them from touching our hair and skin. Their children had not yet developed those filters and naturally there were curious. They asked questions. They felt. They touched. They smelled. They asked Jennifer how come she was black and had a white father. I had to explain to my daughter that Matt chose to be her Daddy after Jerome left, and that he loved her more than all the stars in the sky. I convinced her she was the luckiest of all little girls: she had two Dads: one who loves so her much he wanted to be with her always, and the other too far away to see her everyday. She went around singing: I have two Daddies. Until, that was, she asked the operator to find her other daddy, the black one. It was clear, Jerome's parental rights had to be terminated, ridding of the burden I had bestowed upon him, granting him his wish to be truly free of us. That was to be done back in the States. Jurisdiction dictated.

❦

New Year's eve was a big deal in the Eastern Suburbs. Hell it was a big deal all over the world but took on different meaning for Dorothy who couldn't or wouldn't stop talking about her invitation to the ultra exclusive dinner at the Royal Sydney Golf Club, an-invitation-to-join-members-only establishment in Rose Bay. The entire Archer clan belonged. They had to; they were generations of doctors; had lived in Vaucluse; had sent their children and children's children to Sydney Grammar.

We found out that though Dorothy welcomed us into her home, we were not as welcomed into her life. Jennifer and I were of another pedigree and were best kept in the house. Matt broke the news:

"J. I really don't know how to say this but…"

"But what?"

"Well, you know darls, Dorothy can be quite the …"

I had gotten used to Matt trying to explain and then apologize for his mother and wondered why he was laboring so hard to say exactly what he was trying to convey. He was never one to 'select' his words, not even to protect his mother. He had told me how she had not so much as visit him when he was hospitalized as a child, despite her being a doctor, mind you. I guess she had her patients to whom she had to tend. He had also lamented that despite having more money than they could spend in their lifetime, how she'd make them wear hand-me-downs and what not.

"Matt, what are you trying to say? Quite the what?"

"Well, we can't go with Dorothy and Dad to the New Year's Eve."

I always thought it strange that Matt called his mother Dorothy but his father Dad.

"Shoot, is that all?"

"It's more J."

"More? What more could there be?"

"Well, J. You see Dorothy had always had this thing. She means well but cares too much about what people think."

"How does that make it more?"

"She told me I couldn't take *you*, J."

"Me? What the hell would I do there anyway?"

"I don't think you understand J, it's about your skin color."

"My skin?"

"J, she literally said and I quote, 'you can't have her there, what will people think, I mean she's black?'"

Funny, I never really thought of myself as black, truth be told. I was always Jamaican, a fair-skinned Jamaican, who, if left unbothered by the sun, would be what they'd call high yellow. Besides, I supposed, I had grown up with teachers and lawyers and doctors and heads of government et cetera, et cetera, who look like me, it was hardly necessary to remind myself of by blackness.

In any event, my debut at the Royal Sydney Golf Club was cancelled. I cared less about some high-falluting soiree at the RSGC or any other haven for snobbery than I did about suddenly questioning my skin. Why the hell should my skin limit my horizon or curtail my dreams. Why should my skin color determine access? I wasn't back in Jamaica where the tone of the skin determined the height of success, and even if I were, my café au lait would not have particularly limited me. Hell, I loved my skin and my hair and my nose and all that made me, and though in snow-white Vaucluse I was 'different,' I was no less. I concluded that Matt's mother would not suck the joy out of my life, she wouldn't be granted access to hurt, so I just buried the whole thing and went back to the business of living and loving my café au lait and all.

We, that is, Matt, Jennifer and I, continued living at Dorothy and McMillan's. That is, until we returned from center city Sydney one day to find McMillan putting our belongings, our clothes and suitcases, on the back porch. It was a hint we had to leave then and there. Words were so unnecessary. We moved next door into Jennie's old place. Jennie, God rest her soul, was Matt's Godmother, from whom Matt's mother stole land, literally. I was shocked because I thought that sort of fence-moving maneuver only happened in Jamaica. In any event, Jennie had recently died and Dorothy made sure her kids inherited what she hadn't stolen of Jennie's property. If you had asked me, Jennie's afforded better views of the Sydney Harbour. Perhaps why Dorothy wanted to usurp that valuable bit of real estate from a lonely, family-less old widow.

Would I have done the same?

⤠

I took refuge in the color-blind kindness of Kay and Muriel Wild, German expats who lived on Hopetoune Avenue, across from the Archers. I wasn't in love with their son so there was hardly a reason not to like me just because I had the natural God-given tan so many white folks basked in the sun or artificial lights to achieve, along the way picking up all sorts of skin cancer. Muriel was, I imagined, the Jacquelyn Kennedy Onasis of Australia: beautiful, polished, sophisticated, kind, loving, empathetic and human. At age 90, she still wore a two-piece bathing suit for her daily dips in Parsley Bay. She was graceful, homage to Grace Kelly I told myself. And almost immediately upon meeting her, I wanted to be like her, to talk in the same ambiguous tongue as her, to dress like her, to empathize like her. I wanted to be her. And, I imagined her to be my new mother by choice.

"Julie dawlin," she'd start just about every sentence in a decidedly Lauren Bacall tone, "you mustn't let anyone determine your value my deah."

'Value?' There is no price tag on me, I thought; no über-expensive, très chic brand name. While I might not have then appreciated the value of Muriel's counsel, I knew enough to adore her style, her fashion, her charisma and her poise. I especially adored the way she looked at her husband Kay. If Muriel was Jackie O meet Grace Kelly with a sprinkle of Audrey Hepburn, he was most definitely Cary Grant meet Prince Rainier. He was her admirer, even after 60+ years of marriage.

It was obvious he adored her and she basked in that adoration. I wanted that for me. That was perhaps why my days were spent in the company of Muriel, a woman older than my own grandmother, more sophisticated but older.

✝   ✝   ✝

Lo, children [are] an heritage of the Lord: [and] the fruit of he womb [is his] reward. As arrows [are] mighty in the hand of a mighty man, so [are] children of the youth.

—Psalms 127:3-5

Alas, however, my days with Muriel were numbered, limited to two years. Before long we were packing and readying for our return to the US. It was a sadness peppered with glee as I rather liked the devil with whom I was so comfortable—my own family. The only difference was that it would no longer be Jennifer, Matt and me; we were to be joined by another. I was pregnant—again, deliberately and overjoyed.

However overjoyed we were to return to the States, business detained Matt in Australia. Jennifer and I had gone ahead before the airline personnel could have prevented my growing belly from boarding a near 24-hour flight. Jennifer could scarcely understand why she had to leave her best friend Mara, or why she and I were now sleeping on Dee's sofa bed. A couple months after our arrival in the East Flatbush section of Brooklyn, Sydney Taylor Archer was born on June 8, 1995, the same birth date as my late brother Oin, only 33 years apart.

We had often thought my new daughter a reincarnation of Oin. What might Oin's kids have been like? Would he have married? Whom might he have married? Anyway, Sydney made her grand entry in grand style, all 8lbs 3 ounces and 21 inches of her. She betrayed any blackness, instead boasting red hair, green eyes and skin whiter than that of an albino. I had given birth to a white baby, so white in fact, despite the wrist-bands identifying us as mother and child, a security guard was deployed to escort us to the front desk where another security officer nod in assent when told "yes, this is *her* child." I still remember the look on the nurses' faces when my brother-in-law, black as night, had jokingly told them he was my husband.

Matt arrived a month later and moved us to Bryn Mawr, Pennsylvania. It might have been postpartum depression, it might have been the burdens of getting acquainted with my new city, whatever the cause, nothing I tried eased the pain in my heart; not shopping, not days at the gym, not running. If the rock band U2 was right about "running to stand still," Reggae god Bob Marley must have been talking directly to me when he sang: "yuh running and yuh running and yuh running away, but you can't run away from yourself." It was time to face me, to revisit the crevices in which so much was stashed. Matt insisted and I didn't fight. I was tired of running and getting nowhere or worse, to end up where I'd started. I tried a succession of therapists. Mostly they just sat and stared at me in amazement, as if I were some weird, dirty creature, soiled and stupid, who failed to realize I am the reason for my being there. I was guilty of luring flesh of my blood into my web of sensuality. I was reaping the fruits of my labor, how could I not have understood that? Their stares through judgmental lenses said: consequences meet your actions.

Should you think me ungrateful for not fully appreciating therapy, know that I never gave up on it but for a while I was skeptical *it* could help *me*. You see, my therapist, shrinks, psychologists, whatever their titles, were not like those depicted by Hollywood. There were no plush couches, no reference manuals lining the walls, no mood lighting. Just judgmental assholes I thought were more interested in the salacious and often x-rated recollections of my misfortunes. Surely such tales of incest and molestation and abuse and abandonment were imagined, the ranting of a fanciful woman.

If therapy wasn't to help, maybe an education would. I resumed my education, bettering myself at Temple University in Philadelphia. It was already 1996, more than halfway through the 90s and I was getting no younger. Studying, my girls—and Matt became a singular focus. It paid off: In 1998 I graduated summa cum laude, Top Scholar, with Bill Cosby as the guest speaker.

Yes indeed, me, Julie from Jamaica graduating Top Scholar. I would go onto join an elite group of budding journalists: I, Julie Marie Mignott before Taylor, now Washington and Archer-in-waiting, was a Dow Jones copyediting intern. While my fellow interns went off to places I'd heard of, I ended in Middletown, New York. I nonetheless patted myself on the shoulder, and tried to hide the mortal disappointment when my mother, who had by then moved to Florida, did not use the all-expense paid trip to see her eldest daughter graduate—Top Scholar.

✢ ✢ ✢

*For all that is in the world, the desires of the
flesh and the desires of the eyes and pride in
possession is not from the Father but of the world.*

—1 John 2:16

Having outgrown the apartment in Bryn Mawr, Matt bought a house mere miles away, though worlds apart. We were moving up all right except the mainline mansion Matt had bought was starting to feel more like a plantation than a home. By any upwardly mobile standards it should have been the culmination of a dream: 10 bedrooms, three fireplaces, a 15-ft by 30-ft living room, a formal dining room as large as the living room, a 20-ft by 30-ft kitchen, formal library, rolling formal gardens, and more bathrooms than bottoms. We were perched on North Springmill Road, directly across from Villanova University in one of the most prestigious suburbs of Philadelphia.

A few months there and I understood implicitly why it was called MAINLINE. Though I often imagined Grace Kelly sauntering, or Katherine Herpburn and Cary Grant in Philadelphia Story, *my* stint in Mainline Philadelphia was a little less storied. It was instead filled with stares, glances, overtones, innuendos and intimidation. Like the time I was walking Ginger, our Rhodesian Ridgeback/Boxer mix and a neighbor looked down her nose as she asked, referring to Ginger of course, "so whose is she?" Or when, upon returning from my usual run and eager for a shortcut home, I went through John and Jerry's mega mansion on which contractors and carpenters were busying themselves.

Having reached my neighbors' front door, I slowed to a trot, hoping either would come say hello, as they'd done so often. The contractor, the hired help, was eager and resolute in his approach, determined to stop my intrusion.

"I'm sorry, you can't be here," he advised.

"What?"

"You can't be here, the Rothchilds aren't home."

"Why are you telling me that?"

"Because I'm in charge here and you are not allowed to be here."

"Tell you what, you continue hammering and cleaning up after yourself and I'll be sure to tell Jerry you were a good watch boy. Good boy," I said.

I climbed the fence and was at my front door before the red left his face. The overzealous contractor and the snooty dog walker were hardly enough to make me want to regret living in Villanova. Heck, their antics made for great dinner conversations; *they* were entertaining. The entertainment grew sinister, like a romantic comedy with gore-thirsty Freddie Kruger as the leading man. The police soon began providing unsolicited accompaniment just about every time I, or my visitors of color, ventured out of my circular driveway.

Matt and I had finally had enough when we returned from a weekend trip to find every French door and window broken, toilets and sinks ripped from their cradles and tossed from the second floor, furniture broken, walls smeared and remnants of hate strewn about the house. Worse than the vandalism and its inherent message was the Radnor Police's refusal to lift a finger to even dust for fingerprints.

We moved to Miami at the turn of the Century. (Sounds dramatic, doesn't it?) Anyway, it was a good move; my parents and sisters had already been there for a couple years, and had all bought their own homes. That is, after they'd had enough of living with us in Villanova. South Florida was far friendlier, and closer to my Jamaica which just a little over an hour away.

I quickly found work as the Public Information Officer for the City of North Miami. Not bad. My professional life was shaping up just as my personal life was unraveling. Matt and I were coming unglued even as we enrolled Jennifer and Sydney in one of the most exclusive private schools in Miami, where my daughters were rubbing shoulders with Camelot. Jennifer, not knowing or caring about pedigree, became best friends with Teddy Kennedy Shriver, yes, grandnephew of the late John F. Kennedy, the 35th president of the United States of America. It should have been a beautiful time: career started; girls good and settled (if but temporary); reconnection to my familiar. But as children and career were good-getting-better, my 10-year relationship with Matt came to an end; not a dramatic, drawn out, disturbing end, but an end nonetheless.

Neither Matt nor I were surprised, disappointed but not surprised. It had begun unraveling in Villanova, but we knew we were great friends, and for the sake of the children (or whatever), had been kept up appearances. Behind the appearances though, were scars too deep to bury. At first the allure of an open relationship was intoxicating. I had a steady home life and the freedom to "see" whomever I wanted, whenever

I wanted. Talk about freedom; be careful what you wish for, sometimes the grass is greener on the other side and sometimes it's just artificial turf. In my case, the grass had appeared greener. But no sooner than I tried it out that I found it simply was not what I really wanted. What I wanted most was to feel wanted, needed, valued. I didn't want my cake if I had to devour it too.

Matt's being a great father, great provider, great friend, didn't negate my great need to feel special, I yearned for that sense of belongingness; not ownership or control, you know, belonging to one man who valued and cherished me, like Kay cherished Muriel.

Unfortunately the 'enviable' external life was not reflective of its malnourished internal counterpart. Sadly for Matt, I had somehow learned to say what I wanted, not demand, say. I had learned to say 'when you do that, it makes me feel like this.' But the more I said what I wanted, what I didn't want, the more Matt fantasized about me with Tom, Dick or Harry; the more he wanted me to call him by some conquest's name when we had sex. It was just too much role-playing. The move to Florida was in part an attempt to reconnect, to rediscover what Matt and I first found in each other, exclusive of external stimuli.

We sought couples' therapy. It might have helped if the therapist didn't take on dual roles of counseling us as a couple, *and* each of us individually. Together, Matt and I were told to work on our relationship, to take steps to reinvent, to reinvigorate. Individually, I wondered if the therapist was telling Matt that I was toxic and bad for him, like he was telling me Matt was toxic and no good for me. In the end though, I didn't need a shrink to tell me our shrink was no good for me. I certainly didn't need a shrink that spoke through both sides of his mouth, spewing whatever advice he deemed suited to captive ears as long as the money kept coming. Though I still needed to work on me, work on the relationship was indeed worthless. I was again in search of a new therapist but had just about lowered my expectations. Then, I took a break. Literally. Matt and I separated, with tears but without fanfare, without drama, without regrets. He wanted an open relationship where he shared his conquests and fantasized about mine. I wanted a man to adore me, cherish me, value me; be jealous even. Matt was good to me; he wasn't good for me.

✟　✟　✟

Wives submit yourselves unto the husbands, as unto the Lord. For the husband is the head of the wife, even as Christ is the head of the church: And he is the saviour of the body.

—Ephesians 5:22-23

had scarcely ever been without a man. I've been between men, sometimes quite literally, but hardly ever without one. I sometimes had one while actively looking for another; found a better one while with another; whatever the case, men were never far. For example, when I met Sebastian Santorini on Las Olas Boulevard in downtown Fort Lauderdale. I was with Matt. Though we had buried our relationship, we still had our friendship and we were still parents. And what Matt hated more than he loved the idea of strange men inside me, was throwing away money on rent. Sure he was preparing to go back to Australia but wanted to ensure the girls and I had a place of our own, so there we were meeting our realtor on Las Olas, shopping for a new condo. "Gotta build equity, J, gotta build equity; it's absolutely no good being income rich and asset poor," was his mantra, his admonition.

Anyway, I started telling you about Sebastian, a short, severely balding man with a thick Spanish accent who had apparently waited long enough for Matt to walk into the antique shop before striking a conversation with me.

"Hi, you are beautiful." As conceited as this might sound, I was beginning to forget I was beautiful. I had forgotten about the scores of people back in Seaforth telling my mother I would grow up to be a heart breaker. I remember having my heart broken, I hadn't discovered, or perhaps never consciously owned the power to break hearts.

"Thank you," I said with not the slightest interest in feigning sincerity.

I was surprised I had told him my real name. I usually had some made up moniker for men in whom I had absolutely no interest. The number might have been real, but the name would be made up, that way when they called and asked for, let's say, Sandra, I could say with confidence, "there is no Sandra here, sorry you must have the wrong number." It was easier and more polite, more considerate than brushing them off. Yes, I was all too concerned with bruising their egos or discounting the courage it took to approach a woman.

"I just wanted to let you know I've been watching you for about two blocks now and just had to come over and say hello."

"Well, hello, hope you have a great evening."

"May I give you my card?"

"No worries."

"Sebastian Santorini," he said, extending his hand.

"Julie."

"I hope I'm not bothering you but I would love to take you to dinner."

"I'm sorry but..."

"You don't have to say yes now, but I would love to hear from you."

"OK, might just do that."

"You are absolutely..."

"I'm sorry I have to go, nice meeting you Sebastian Santorini."

A few days later, Matt was driving me to meet Sebastian Santorini, who according to his business card was Managing Director for First Union Asset Management. Matt had driven me to meet conquests before, but that time it was different. It was different because whatever happened on the date, I wouldn't have to recall in exacting details whilst Matt and I were having sex.

Sebastian Santorini, a self-made man originally from Argentina, was quite the charmer. Before long, I was having more than dinner with him and instead of Matt and I shopping for a condo, it was Sebastian and I shopping for a home. I had just about given up the temporary apartment and had all but moved in with the virtual stranger. Maybe it was his abundant undiluted attention I so craved. Adoration. Maybe it was feeling loved in a grown-up sort of way. Maybe it was feeling valued when he showed up at my office with long-stem roses and chocolate, not just for me but for my female coworkers as well. Maybe it was Sebastian showing up in the brand new Mercedes Benz E430 I had admired just the week before. Maybe it was what I needed then.

Whatever he was selling, I was buying. You would have too. Let's see, a two-story Venetian Causeway condo overlooking Biscayne Bay and downtown Miami—with Heavyweight Champion Lennox Lewis as a neighbor; a Mercedes Benz; long-stem roses; dinners at the best restaurants, even when they were at capacity and we didn't have a reservation. I was a glutton for external living, it showed I had value, could be validated. I was indeed saddened when the abundant undiluted attention became overwhelming. The surprise encounters at my office were becoming ominous, perhaps because even when I had unannounced meetings in undisclosed locations, Sebastian would show up at the undisclosed locations at the conclusion of the unannounced meetings.

In fact, the police, including the chief and his second in command, gave me a code, and all I had to do was call and say "red roses" and they'd know I was in eminent danger at home. My mother developed the annoying but reassuring habit of calling me every morning, just to say, "oh, you alive." Things started turning really sour at the Marlins Hotel on Miami Beach. Sebastian and I had gone there for a drink, as we had done so many Saturday nights. And like every other Saturday night, I engaged the room, chatting with Tom, Dick and Harry.

Eric LaSalle was among the Tom, Dick and Harry and as an actor on the then red-hot ER, he was engaging *and* recognizable. Sebastian must have felt threatened because he lurked closer than usual. So close in fact, his breath fanned the back of my neck. I guessed I was a little too enamored with Hollywood Eric or he with me, but Sebastian had had enough and wanted to leave. If Sebastian had simply said he wanted to leave, perhaps I would have happily obliged. However, he chose instead to grab my left arm, though I was sure anyone paying attention might have mistaken his malice for affection. I felt dread. Not the same as I had felt with my uncle George or my uncle Norburt. But dread nonetheless, like I was about to vanish, never to be heard from again. My mind said go, but my feet said hell no.

He grabbed harder, all the while with a smile on his face. When my feet still didn't budge nor my gaze averted from Hollywood Eric, Sebastian dug his fingernails into my flesh and twisted. I might have winced but I was done being coerced. I was not going to give him the satisfaction of telling me what to do. I was also determined to not vanish, not to have become a 'have you seen this woman' statistic. My eyes, filled with tears left Eric's face and fell to the floor. 'Do I scream for help?' 'Do I run?' When I looked up again, Eric was gone, and within seconds, two mammoths for bouncers grabbed Sebastian under each armpit, only then did he release the grip on my arm. My skin was broken, giving way to fresh red blood. I had seen blood before. Sebastian tried to protest but his pleas simply fell on unsympathetic ears. I watched as he was escorted, more like handled, feet dangling about two feet above the floor, and was tossed onto Collins Avenue. Months passed before Sebastian charmed me into another dinner. His apologies were overwhelming if not entirely sincere. I accepted when I didn't truly believe.

The whisper in my gut turned into a full roar but still I chose to ignore it. I went back to 1000 Venetian Causeway, the apartment that had so soothed my soul, so satisfied my need for status. Sebastian proved he was sorry for losing his temper and things started well. Until, of course he had done something else for which he needed to apologize. Actually, he had done several things for which he needed forgiveness: I had again left but my addiction to the life he afforded kept me believing he really hadn't meant to hurt me. I kept going back.

I went back after he held my clothes hostage on one my 'I can't take this anymore departures.' He relinquished them only after I had threatened him, not with incarceration or bodily harm, but I had threatened to call the president of the First Union and the *Miami Herald*. He had kept my black leather trousers he thought was "too sexy" to be worn outside his watch. I even went back after he had driven me, against my will to a hotel in Boca Raton where I spent the night not sure what he had in mind. Yes, I even went back after that episode, only I was becoming 'smarter.' One evening I was driving across the Venetian Causeway towards South Beach. I had just exited the tollbooth when I saw Sebastian driving in the opposite direction. He waved at me, beckoning me to stop. I did, and there we were, talking from our respective car, like cops often do. It was all a bit silly, sitting in our cars, talking like police officers. Sebastian parked his Mercedes while I stayed in the Land Rover Matt had bought me, wanting to ensure our safety from the notorious Miami drivers. "It's a good solid car, J," he had said, pleasingly.

Anyway, Sebastian walked up to my car. We exchanged pleasantries. It had been a while since the 'kidnapping.' Sebastian invited me to dinner, to which I agreed, but only if we took our respective cars. Last time I got in his car, I ended up in Boca Raton, with only fear as my real companion.

Suffice it to say, Sebastian did not like my suggestion. Almost instantaneously he want from apologetic to menacing, the other less attractive side to his coin. He climbed up onto the running board of the Land Rover and reached in and grabbed the key, determined to dislodge it from the ignition. What he had failed to realize was that I had the car in drive and therefore the key could not have been removed. Sebastian was none too happy and lunged even further into my car, his feet dangling out the window, and he tried even more desperately to ram the gear into park. I did what my gut told me to, for once, and I accelerated with Sebastian dangling from my window. I sped up with enough determination to show I meant business, but he just clung there, spread across my lap and more determined to put my car into park. I braked as hard as I could, causing the SUV to sway before coming to a stop. That sent Sebastian up against the dash and I supposed he had learned his lesson. He climbed down but rather than go on about his business, he got in his car and started chasing me along the Venetian Causeway.

I reached for my cell phone and called 911. The operator told me to find a well lit and preferably busy place with people around. That was just about impossible on the Venetian Causeway where people remained locked behind mile-high walls, or in their mansions in the sky. I drove back to the toll-booth but was asked to move aside so the other cars could get by. If I felt dread during the Marlins Hotel incident, I was sure I was to die, unceremoniously on the Venetian Causeway. Ever the stubborn one, I disobeyed the toll collector and rather than pull aside, I raced through the toll lane and across the drawbridge.

The SUV swayed as if to topple as I screeched to a stop at the Grand Hotel, all the while screaming, "he's going to kill me, he's going to kill me." I had not even had the prescience to remove the key from the ignition; I had barely put the car in park when I ran into the bar where at least there would be witnesses to me death. The police eventually showed up, but rather than arrest Sebastian, they simply looked at his business card and told him to leave me alone unless he in fact wanted to end up behind bars—and ruin *his* life.

He might have been told to leave me alone, but *I* still went back after more rounds of flowers and jewelry and all the things meant to appease a greedy, 'licky licky' woman. I went back wishing things had changed but was always plotting my escape; looking for a way out had they not changed—for the better. And at first, they had changed. Sebastian was a loving, caring, supportive boyfriend. Until one Saturday morning I had had the nerve, the audacity to want to go to the gym—alone. He had insisted on going with me, as he had done for *everything* else. It was as if I had grown a permanent shadow though even shadows went to sleep at nights—well mostly. And you know what they used to say: *trust no shadow after dark.*

Before long a full-blown argument had erupted. I never lose an argument. A physical fight without a pocketful of corn-meal was another thing. I tried to wrangle my grandmother's scarf from the enraged lunatic. He won. He placed the scarf, my Mama's scarf, in the kitchen sink and set it on fire as if to send a warning, a message, that obedience and surrender are most appreciated. Independence was neither welcomed nor encouraged.

He might not have known my grandmother had given me that scarf, and that it was my link to her. He might not have known that burning it would have been worse than a physical blow. He knew it would devastate. He made it up with a trip to see my grandmother—back in Jamaica. I was charmed. I was convinced. On September 1, 2000, we flew to see my grand-mother, the next best thing to having her scarf.

I had the video camera rolling as we pulled up to Pops and Mama's, fully expecting Pops' head to bob and weave as he tried to make out the strangers walking down his driveway.

There was to be no bobby or weaving. I could see Pops laying on the lounge, but there was no movement. He just laid there, almost motionless. With video camera still rolling I got out of the car and approached. Still, he didn't move. His head wasn't bobbing to see to whom the approaching feet belonged. He wasn't dead, but it was obvious he was courting death. When he finally spoke, his pulpit voice was reduced to a whimper and he barely managed to say, between tears, "gyal mi a dead."

"Stop talk foolishness Pops."

"No Julie, mi a dead man. Mi a go meet mi Lawd."

He cried out loud. I cried hard.

"Where's Mama?"

"She gone a Seaforth to call Norburt dem."

"Which part a Seaforth?"

"Sister Morgan," he said in a whisper.

Sebastian stayed with Pops, the stranger he had just met and most certainly didn't understand as I drove back to Seaforth to find my grandmother and save her from a five-mile walk back to her dying husband. I borrowed a phone and called Winsome and Dee to alert them of their father's condition. They said they'd make arrangements.

Pops was in excruciating pain that made him recoil at the touch. He had no interest in the Sanka or Maxwell House coffee I brought him; or the Mach 3 razors and special shaving cream; or the Calvin Klein Obsession. He didn't tell me to hide them, his special things from abroad from his good-for-nothing son Stephen, who though he was grown, had preferred the shelter of free rent—and Mama's mothering.

It wasn't like the scores of times, when longing for a visit from his children Pops called abroad to say he was dying. There was no 'boy crying wolf' that time; my grandfather was dying. Mama wiped his tears and forced her own back in. We got Pops dressed and took him to the doctor in Morant Bay. It was a harrowing drive. He cried at each bump, each pothole. In other words, he cried all the way. The doctor was sensitive to the urgency of Pops' condition—or was it the lure of crisp American $100 bills. Whatever, he took Pops ahead of the scores of people moaning and groaning, writhing and bleeding in his waiting room. He gave Pops no diagnosis, just enough medicine to ease his transition, quiet his cries. My grandfather slept soundly through the bumps and potholes back to his house. Pops was eased. I was relieved.

Sebastian and I took him back to the doctor for more injections each day I remained in Jamaica. The injections weren't to cure what ailed him; they were to make his last days bearable. And with each shot, he was numb enough to sit up, to joke, to let me shave him, bathe him, make him coffee, cut his nails, comb his hair, talk. When I had to leave for Miami, I told Pops I was coming back for us to play football. He laughed and the hug was no longer painful for him so it lingered.

"Gyal, you not coming back to see me."

"A lie dat, mi soon come man."

"Is alright, mi going to meet mi God, Julie."

"You not going anywhere Pops. God not ready fi yuh yet."

"Ah mi gyal. Mi ready, mi mek mi peace."

I didn't want him to see me cry but my wants and my heart's needs were not in agreement. The more I cried, the more he tried to comfort me between his own tears. He grabbed my right knee with the grip of Samson. And he didn't let go. The camera rolled, capturing every second of a grandfather's refusal to let go and a granddaughter's wishes for life—eternal. Sebastian finally peeled Pops' hand from my knee, and just like that, I was watching Pops and Mama from the rear view mirror of a rented car.

Mere days after Sebastian and I returned to Miami, I woke up at 10:15am on Saturday, September 16, one day before my 32nd birthday. I had been dreaming that I was fluffing Pops' pillows on his grave and called Winsome's house. I knew she was in Jamaica, by her father's side, but wanted to get word to her via her daughter Brittany. Brittany didn't wait for me to tell her my dream; she had had news of her own.

"So did you hear?"

"No, but I know what you're going to tell me," I said trying to understand why I couldn't cry and wondering if others had had the same dream or anything similar.

"Pops passed this morning."

"I know, he said goodbye."

Like my brother 17 years earlier, Pops, three months shy of his 89th birthday, was dead and had been put on display at the Seaforth branch of the Church of God of Prophecy. It was Saturday, September 23. Even those of his kids who had all but forsaken him were there to pay their respects, to mourn. Mama was concerned how he looked; she said he didn't look like himself. He didn't.

He wasn't Pops the pastor.

He wasn't Pops the overseer.

He wasn't Pops the grandfather.

He just wasn't himself.

He was cold to the touch.

Unresponsive.

Dead.

Pops had left the body. I wondered if he could hear my eulogy, my gratitude for him and *all* he was, all he did. Sebastian and I left the burial, not to leave or because it was unbearable, but to go see the path where decades earlier George had first tried to rape me.

I had to go say goodbye to the beginning. The path was long overgrown, impassable. It could no longer be entered, be penetrated, be used. It was no longer a shortcut to a life ruined. Its usefulness had apparently long expired. Strange. And say what you will, despite the hellish nature of our relationship, Sebastian was put in my life for a reason: because of his brutish, controlling, abusive ways, I got to see my grandfather before he died. I got to say goodbye to the path, to the beginning. I had seen, firsthand, the demise of the path; it had not seen mine.

✝ ✝ ✝

And they brought young children to him, that he should touch them: And [his] disciples rebuked those that brought [them]. But when Jesus saw [it], he was much displeased, and said unto them, suffer the little children to come unto me, and forbid them not: For such is the kingdom of God.

—Mark 10:13-14

Wouldn't you know: Turned out that as we were in Jamaica burying my Pops, my sister's husband was back in Florida burying his penis in my 11 year-old child. At first we all thought that Jennifer's "acting up" was her way of grieving a grandfather she did not know, but grieving nonetheless, if purely out of empathy. I didn't understand why she had taken a liking to all things gothic, especially the black clothing, spiked hair, black nails, black lips, and just overall blackness. (She had always been so preppy.)

Jennifer had experimented with phases though none as severe as 'goth,' and I just thought it was another step in her self-discovery as she raced toward adolescence. Like me, Jennifer was always big for her age. It seemed she had always been 5'9". Even her pediatrician in Villanova had wanted to test her for Marfan's Syndrome, that genetic disorder of the connective tissue. People with Marfan's Syndrome tend to be unusually tall. It was widely speculated that President Abraham Lincoln had Marfan's Syndrome. In any event, Dr. Bomze was fascinated by Jennifer's development, and was especially intrigued when she started her period at age 9. He had said that black girls tend to develop faster than their white counterparts, but was nonetheless surprised by the early onset of her period. We didn't test for Marfan's Syndrome. I was big. Members of my family, especially the males, were big. The average uncle stood 6'2". And though Jennifer's father barely cleared 5'7", I just took it for granted that my daughter was predominantly of me, my DNA.

My girls were especially close to my sister Mawma and her kids, as it should have been. Mawma and I had remained virtually inseparable. We knew whence we came, sleeping in the same bed, wearing the same clothes, literally, eating the same food and sharing the same parenting. We were determined not to let the hassles of foreign life rob us of our childhood closeness, and raised our kids more like siblings than cousins. Lorraine, Mawma's first born, was like my own daughter. In fact, people would've been hard pressed to say which child belonged to which mother. And my sister's twins, Cory and Cody, became my twins by proxy though I had refused to hold them at birth. They were premature and barely weighed two pounds each, making them look fragile. They grew though, better than expected for preemies, and though they didn't suffer any major setbacks, they had their share of medical mishaps.

In any event, I was telling you how close the cousins were, and that either I had them all or Mawma had them all. My girls had even lived with Mawma when we first moved to Florida and before I decided on Miami versus Broward County. Back then weekends often meant I had seven children: my two (Sydney and Jennifer); Mawma's three (Lorraine, Cody and Cory); Stephanie's two (Andrea and Dylan). We often wondered what onlookers thought, with mouths agape, as I pulled in front of

Sunrise Cinemas and all seven children plus Jennifer's friends climbed from the Land Rover from which Sebastian had dangled. The poor car, it was a seven-seater, not Noah's Ark.

There were similar scenes at the beach or at the mall. And when we went to Universal Studios in Orlando, we damn near needed an entire floor of the hotel. Mealtime was more like the Last Supper with all the disciples in tow.

⁓

Matt was closer to setting an actual date for his repatriation. He lingered to ensure I was safe from Sebastian and his form of love. Matt had seen, on multiple occasions, the effects of Sebastian's love and wanted nothing more than for me to be free of it. He had seen me depressed, he had seen me deflated; he had seen me defeated. And when I had begged him to help me rid myself of the addiction to Sebastian, Matt had simply obliged, offering advice, love, support, and most important, he refrained from judging. He had even stayed to settle the girls and I in our own apartment overlooking Biscayne Bay in Miami. Fort Lauderdale, actually no part of Broward County was for me. He stayed with us while he tried to narrow a return date. He was the girls' primary caregiver while I worked and while I was on the prowl for whatever next-in-line man who was absolutely the one to wean me from Sebastian. Next in line turned out to be Stephan Breunig, whom I met at Touch on Lincoln Road. Matt and I had gone there for drinks, as we'd done so many times before. We had barely been seated when I noticed the salt-and-pepper haired man noticing me. As far as he knew, though, I was 'with' Matt.

Matt noticed me noticing the salt-and-pepper noticing me; we had done *that* dance before, so Matt knew when to give me space. He did what any considerate friend would do; he went to the bathroom. Matt had barely left when the salt-and-pepper glided over (I swear he didn't walk, just sort of floated), and with the thickest accent said, "Hi, I'm Stephan." No he wasn't a French Stephan; he was an Austrian Stephan. Stephan Breunig, of Matt's height, less bulky and with black-framed glasses. And the more he spoke, the more he sounded like Arnold Schwarzenegger. After all, both men did share the same mother tongue. Stephan Breunig, the Viennese who preferred Miami's warm winters, maintained an apartment of the Venetian Causeway. By the time Matt got back from the bathroom, I was hooked, infatuated, on to the next.

Matt prolonged his stay in Miami, partly to see how brightly and quickly that flame would burn, but mostly to provide stability to the girls. He was right. Before long I was off to Vienna. Stephan's winter stint was over though my infatuation had just begun and was already in overdrive. One trip turned into two, three, four, five. Flying was getting too much, I *did* have children and a job! Stephan and I decided I would move to Vienna. That is, after I had agreed to marry him. He took me to Jamaica to celebrate the engagement.

When we got back from my beloved Jamaica, we busied ourselves combing Vienna and surrounds for American schools for my girls. Things were going well. I had even gotten Matt's blessings and was looking forward to life in Austria. Mostly. I had grown to hate the regimented life of Stephan Breunig. Everything was on a schedule: layout banana, croissant and tea the night before for breakfast the following morning; arrange all the shoes in a row and polishing even the ones not being worn anytime soon; lunch at the same time; same routes.

It was to be a life devoid of deviation, of spontaneity.

I had nonetheless convinced myself, I could be the regimented wife until, he made *my* schedule: awake at 7am; breakfast at 7:15; shower at 7:45; Berlitz at 9. 'What?' I thought, I was the same Julie who had flown to Vienna to see Stephan, a couple months after meeting him in a glorified bar. I was the same Julie about to uproot my girls and plant them in a strange new land. I didn't do schedules. That simple. We tried to compromise. Matt even brought the girls Vienna to see me. When they arrived, it was to a Julie he didn't recognize, a Julie who left her girls and Matt in the apartment recently vacated by the death of Stephan's mother.

Stephan and I stayed in *his* apartment miles away. My heart still aches at the sight of my Sydney crying, wanting her mom who was going off again—with a man du jour. Stephan had no tolerance for crying children, not even those who had to be pried off their mothers going off with rigid men. I can still hear Stephan telling me my Syd was a big girl who was crying only to manipulate me. The following day Matt took the girls for a stroll down St. Stephansplatz, the main pedestrian drag in the heart of Vienna. I was to join them for the day. Having arrived ahead of schedule and ever the one to make the girls feel independent, grown up, Matt had gone off to browse some window and had left Jennifer and Sydney, by themselves, in the newly-opened Starbucks. Syd got separated from Jennifer. Their recollection of the dread they felt was unbearable.

"Mom, I looked up and I couldn't see Jennifer. All I saw were these huge white people. And when I tried to ask for help, none of them spoke English." Jennifer was just as terrified she had lost her baby sister and there it was, I was comforting some control freak while my children were absolutely suffering. That was simply unacceptable, no matter the level of self-absorption. Matt had had enough too, he went directly back to Sydney while the girls and I returned to Miami.

I had long suspected Jennifer and Syd felt more protected, more stable with Matt. Their constant was gone, to the other end of the world, and they were left with an erratic mother with uncontrollable urges. They longed for him, as did I really. So we all went to see Matt in Australia. He had bought a beautiful apartment in Glebe, minutes from Center City Sydney. It was decorated for a man, by a man, so the first thing I did was redecorate. I added comfort, femininity and best of all function. It was like the old time, the good old time before all the voyeuristic crap had seeped in.

For a full thirty days, we were a family again. Whole. The girls were enrolled in school and had obviously loved being around Matt. I wanted to believe it was because he was the more lenient, sensible, flexible, logical one. But really he just provided love and stability and consistency. Not a parade of Tom, Dick or Harry. And as hard as the decision was, I returned to Miami, without my girls.

A year went by before I went back to visit my kids. I'd spent 30 days with my kids in one year. The visit was fleeting and it felt like just as I'd disembarked at Kingsford Smith Airport only to get back on the plane heading back to Miami.

I was again leaving without my kids, but with the knowledge that things couldn't remain as they were. I might not have known better before or just chose to be selfish. Either way old time people always tell yuh fi lawn fi do better before too late causen seh time nuh wait fi nobody.

Translation: Learn to do better before too it's too late because time waits for nobody.

Meaning: Too many people live with what ifs and why 'nots,' having squandered every opportunity to fix things, delaying remediation for another, more convenient time when self is sufficiently satisfied.

I sent for my girls, and knew it absolutely ripped Matt's heart out. But we had never had a custody agreement, didn't see the need for one when we knew what was better for our girls: choice. It worked for us; the girls could go see Matt whenever they chose, just as they could come live with me whenever they chose. They had freedom. They had always chosen better and by the time they came home, I knew better. I often asked for their forgiveness for being a lousy mother, though they have always lied and assured me there is nothing to forgive.

"Mom, you did the best you could," Jennifer would comfort. "You can't expect a carpenter to build a house with a needle and thread, just as you can't expect a barber to cut your hair with a hammer. Besides, if you weren't who you were, we wouldn't be who we are."

Syd was often less abstract in her consolation, saying, "We never wanted for anything Mom, we were always comfortable, and we got to see the world." My children always said things that helped ease my conscience, lessen the sting, until Syd confessed, in one of our knee-to-knee-tell-me-what-you-don't-like-that-

I'm-doing sessions: "When we were smaller, I used to imagine Jennifer was my mom!"

⤎

I was already married to my newest conquest, an English man named Peter Mansfield, when Jennifer and Sydney returned from Australia. I often joked that I've been trying to conquer the world, one man at time. Well, you know what they say about truths cloaked in jokes. Anyway, my girls had come back to a new stepfather, who though a complete stranger, was good to them and made sure they felt at home, comfortable. He took them to and from school, cooked their meals, became their friend. The road to friendship wasn't a straight one though; it had some twists and turns. There was the time when Peter asked Syd what she wanted for dinner. She was a little curly-haired girl who had always known exactly how she wanted to be treated. She had become incensed with Peter's simple question, "what would you like for dinner?"

"Oh, I don't know."

"What you mean you don't know?"

"Just like I said. I'm not sure what I'm in the mood for."

"Well how about fish?"

"I don't eat fish."

"What about shrimp?"

"Unfortunately I don't eat that either."

"Well what do you eat?"

"Food."

"What kind of food?"

"Oh the kind I like."

"Well what would you like tonight?"

"Not sure really."

"Well I'll leave you to think about it."

Peter left Syd, hair like a lion's mane, wild and all over the place swaying on the swing he had attached to the oak tree in the front yard. I had watched the exchange from the kitchen window of our Bohemian Coconut Grove house. It was a house that lent itself to the leanings of a nomadic mother and her children I thought. Made of entirely Dade County Pine, the house had withstood many of its 1920s counterparts. We had painted the exterior black, a color that had made the house almost invisible from the street. It was further camouflaged by the massive oak tree, and by the black bamboo and mango trees. It was all so tropical; it could have fit in seamlessly in Jamaica, except of course, for the extreme black on the exterior. There were plenty of windows through which rays of sunlight streamed. It was a comfortable house, made habitable by Peter and his desires to please his new family. Anyway, there I was watching the interaction between my new husband and his new stepdaughter. Though I couldn't hear the conversation, I knew by the way Syd knotted her brow, locked her teeth and folded her arms; things hadn't gone so well.

"What's up with my little Syd?" I asked as I extended my arms to embrace her.

"I don't like the way he behaves. He was asking me what I wanted for dinner and I said I don't know, and he just left."

"Well, maybe he doesn't know what you'd like for dinner Syd, which is why he asked."

She hung her head in silence and she didn't force the swing in any direction, she just swayed slowly, whichever way the swing dictated.

"Well my Syd, maybe he was just trying to get to know you baby."

"Well mother, that's no way to get to know me, walking off like that!"

"But Sydney, you have to remember..."

"Mom, I don't like the way he just walked off. He should have stayed and learned what I like to eat. I *don't* like to be treated like that!"

And with that, Sydney Taylor Archer stormed off, leaving the swing to sway whichever way it pleased. We all went out to eat that night, giving Sydney free range to choose.

───৯───

Sydney and Jennifer were close, not in age; they were six years apart. Not in looks either, Jennifer was black and Sydney was at best racially ambiguous if not white. But they always chose to sleep in the same bed, even when they didn't need to. Jennifer was a good big sister, well, when she wasn't busy convincing Syd that she was adopted. Or that I found her by a trash bin and felt sorry for her so I kept her. Yep, Jennifer was a great big sister when she wasn't busy drawing a smiley face on Syd's behind, an eye on each cheek and a mouth across both, and bribing her to hoist her dress so that all the dinner guests, including Matt's colleagues from work, could get a good view. There was also the time Jennifer tried to kill a then two-month-old Syd. We were still in Bryn Mawr and Sydney was having an afternoon nap. I was surprised the nap had lasted as long and had sent Jennifer to check on her baby sister.

"She's still sleeping Mommy."

"Oh good, that means I can finish braiding your hair."

Another thirty minutes or so went by and still not a sound from Syd who normally slept about 40 minutes max. I went to check and found all the pillows from my bed stacked on top of Syd—in her crib. The pillows had apparently grown wings because Jennifer had no idea how they all found themselves stacked on top of her new sister.

But it wasn't all attempted murder and manipulation, Jennifer actually loved taking care of her baby sister, I think. Remember, Syd later told me she sometimes thought of Jennifer as her mother, when I was off with some Tom, Dick or Harry. They were each other's safety *and* stability; they were the only constant in their lives. They grew inseparable, and despite the age difference, were each other's rock. It was especially hard on Syd when Jen was Baker Acted at Miami Children's Hospital. Like I told your earlier, Jennifer had changed, and I had put it down to normal teenage angst.

⎯⎯↶

One evening after dinner, Jennifer asked me into their room as she had something to tell me. She climbed onto the bed and got into a fetal position, tears streaming into the white sheets.

"What's the matter baby?"

"I don't know how to tell you this Mom."

"Tell me what Jen, you know I'm here for you, so tell me what?"

"Leroy had sex with me?"

"Leroy what? What are you talking about? When?"

I could see my questions were overwhelming her so I shut up and just cradled her.

She cried so hard I could feel her every heartbeat. My child felt like a rag doll in my arms and she heaved and cried, as did I, almost perfectly synchronized, as if choreographed. You could say I knew exactly how she felt, but could hardly console her or ease her own pain.

"Tell me what happened baby."

"He had sex with me three times, when I was eleven. That's why we don't want to go there anymore."

"Syd," I bellowed. "Pass me the phone Syd."

Jennifer did not want me to release her, nor did I want to. I held her and we swayed as if sitting in some invisible rocking chair.

She cried till her eyes were swollen shut, and when she finally fell asleep in my arms, I gently eased away so not to disturb her. I tried to call my sister. I tried to call my mother. Nothing came out of me. Peter came home to find me curled in a corner, watching Jen sleep. He knew instantly something was very wrong. Not wanting to rouse Jen, we went outside where I told him what was just told to me. He went from shocked to vengeful in two seconds flat. He wanted to exact punishment, not at all caring about the ramifications on his own freedom. He flew inside and rummaged about for his keys. His rage was so blinding he had forgotten where he put them, though he had quite literally just arrived home. He went to the kitchen. He slammed the cupboard door as if to register his disappointment he hadn't accidentally put them in a glass. He looked in the fridge. He went to the bathroom. He went to our bedroom.

He called out for me as he entered the girls' bathroom. Jennifer was curled up on the floor, still clutching the empty bottle of Tylenol PM. She had swallowed every single pill and was waiting to die. We didn't wait for an ambulance, and miraculously Peter remembered his keys were still in his pocket. He put Jennifer in the passenger seat of his car and we raced her to Mercy Hospital just minutes from our house. They hurried her in and pumped her stomach after giving her some black ink-like substance. I later learned it was activated charcoal. It made her lips jet black and scary, like an exaggeratedly made up zombie in a no-budget horror flick.

They immediately transported her to Miami Children's Hospital, because despite her size, she was still a child. I prayed and wished and promised God that if he let me keep Jennifer, I would be as dutiful as any. The nerves in my belly finally relaxed when they told us Jennifer would be physically okay. I knew in that moment, or so I thought, how my mother, had felt when Oin rejected the water she tried to pour down his throat. Unfortunately, because my daughter had attempted to take her own life, she had to be admitted to the mental ward for evaluation and observation, and to keep her from succeeding with the threat of harming herself or anyone else.

I couldn't stay with my Jen, I had to leave and return during normal visiting hours. She was now a ward of the institution; she was suicidal if not homicidal. The next morning I went to see Jennifer, she had a wild, disconnected, empty look in her eyes, as though the eyes were there but everything else had vacated. Her lips were still black from the charcoal and she looked all at once scared and embarrassed. I held her and she did not want to talk. She was stripped of belts, shoelaces, jewelry; she had been stripped of anything that could have been cajoled into taking a life. A series of doctors paraded their 'findings' and recommendations. "If you sign here we will get her started on anti-depressants," one doctor said. I declined, of course, because I knew all too well that matters of molestation, rape or incest could hardly be medicated with Prozac, Zoloft or any other pharmaceutical meant to numb so the subject doesn't become a burden on those around them. My child was not depressed, she wasn't schizophrenic; she was *raped*. Her trust was betrayed. Her path was interrupted and no amount of drugs would have fixed that; drugs might have camouflaged the pain but they most definitely would not have kept the memories from ravaging her mind, nor would they have kept resulting emotional baggage from materializing and burdening her.

Jennifer was seen by a series of experts, the first of whom advised that because of her age the crime was reported to the police and Department of Children & Families. Ironically, she and I had been down that road years earlier in New York. Only now, we knew the predator, and immediately I thought he might be one and the same: New York and Florida. It must have been my sister's husband (then boyfriend) who caused my infant child's vaginal skin to peel.

Jennifer would spend days in the mental ward and was released only when we agreed to outpatient therapy. (Like I would have considered anything else.) I knew first-hand the ravages of such acts.

DCF investigated. They questioned Jennifer and Syd together.

They questioned Jennifer.

They questioned Syd.

I was NOT allowed to be present for parts of the interviews.

Syd asked me if it was true that Leroy had sex with Jennifer. I said yes, and tried my best to explain to a five year-old child what it all meant.

Both my girls were then introduced to intense therapy, and DCF forwarded the case to Broward County Sherriff's Office (BSO). BSO and DCF interviewed the 'subject.'

They interviewed the subject's wife, my sister.

Jennifer and I met with BSO officers who laid out the course of action and its possible conclusion: Leroy will be arrested and charged with statutory rape. He would be tried and Jennifer would be asked to testify. He stood a good chance of being convicted and imprisoned and forever be labeled a sex offender. Jennifer wept and asked to leave. She asked what would happen to Mawma and Lorraine and Cody and Cory. She wanted to talk to her psychologist. Despite my best offer of support aimed at convincing Jen to testify, to not assume the guilt for something an adult had done *to* her, she simply did not want to re-live the nightmare, an most certainly not before an audience. At a follow up meeting, Jennifer told the BSO detectives she didn't want my sister and her kids to suffer.

Jennifer wanted them to have a normal life, even if her own would forever be altered. Mawma said she was confused but grateful *her* family would remain in tact; at least until she completed her nursing degree, she would take her kids and leave the child rapist. I tried to forgive Leroy seeing as though he himself was a victim of repeated childhood rape. His mother left for New York, and had left him with some strange man who began raping him at age nine. It was hard, still is, though I most certainly don't have a patent of suffering and abuse, I chose not to do to others what was done to me. I remembered the feeling of helplessness and shame and guilt and loss of dignity and hopelessness and hurt and pain and despair and rejection and worthlessness. Why would I chose to inflict any of that on another human being, why would I want anyone to know the sheer hell? Then I remembered I could not, try as I might have, wish as I might have, expect people to behave or feel as I do.

I eventually accepted that I did not have the right, after all, to demand that my sister left her husband the child rapist, the betrayer of trust; that would have to come from her. It couldn't be forced on her like he had forced himself on my daughter.

My sister has been a nurse for some years now and has had another child with her husband. That child she's named Leroy, Jr. I've told her of my disappointment; I've told her that tried as I did, I could not forget what Leroy has done to my child, her niece. I've told her I did not want him included in any family function. I told her he needed to seek the help he so desperately needs. I've told her that he has affected the way I respond to her. I've told her he is no role model for her teenage boys. I've told her I want her to ensure Leroy has not propositioned Lorraine, their first child. I told her I want to help her find the strength to expect more of and for herself. I so want her to find the courage to finally say enough. I want more than anything for her to not condone, to not cultivate the culture of complicity. I want her to finally realize that she has been playing Russian Roulette with her life: though she and Leroy had been married since the birth of their first child, it has never stopped him from engaging in unprotected sex with women other than her. In fact, every time my sister gave birth to another of his children, some other woman also gave birth: there were twins, Janet and Jeanette, the same age as Lorraine. There was the other set of twins, boys, the same age as my sister's twins Cory and Cody. And Leroy had even propositioned my sister Stephanie's daughter, Andrea. He had wanted to know if she wanted him to do to her what he had done to Jennifer.

I wondered what will be the straw for my sister; what will be her 'too much?'

✞   ✞   ✞

Therefore we are buried with him by baptism into death: that like as Christ was raised up from the dead by the glory of the Father, even so we also should walk in newness of life.

—Romans 6:4

In case you were wondering Peter and I divorced after seven years of marriage. Remember, only *true* salvation lasts forever. And now, the good days far outnumber the bad, but on the bad days no river of tears can silence the noise in my head, no amount of spirits can keep the demons out of my bed. All is not lost though, I've learned to own dignity and self worth and that value Muriel had talked about. I've learned to love, really love. Most of all I've learned to shake the shackles of shame, and to assign it to those who've earned it: the predators in my own family. I've learned to talk about my abuse without fear of condemnation and marginalization. I've learned to live outside myself, and have started a charity, Give Me Dignity.

Perhaps the most valuable lesson is learning to never, ever speak to my uncles who abused me, to no longer be controlled by their abuse, to not care what my family might think of my decision to no longer bear the burdens of secrecy, the burdens of ensuring a family name remains in tact. For years I talked to my abusers, considered them family, even socialized with them. I think they have a term for that: Stockholm Syndrome described as a "paradoxical psychological phenomenon" in which victims express empathy and have positive feelings toward their offenders, sometimes to the point of defending them. I now treat them as they deserve to be treated, with disgust, that is, when I think of them at all.

I've learned I've done nothing to tarnish or in any way diminish my name, but instead, take comfort in the hope that the next generations will take pride in knowing the cycle of abuse can be broken. I am but one survivor among too many to continue the silence that breeds the sort of systemic abuse, the silence that tells the predators 'it's okay, that by our silence we approve of your predation.' Four of eight uncles have abused their nieces and other female relatives. Some have even abused own daughters. Cousins have abused their siblings. I don't care for pity; nothing good ever comes from that useless emotion. However, if you're enraged enough start a dialogue, talking *does* help.

In the many, many years of therapy, one shrink jokingly said I should write a book and I should title it "The Men in My Life." Well I have written a book, but you guessed; I changed the title. They are not the men in my life. They are the men who've altered the course of my life, but most definitely they live on the outskirts, outside my lens. Another therapist at the Journey Institute in Miami asked me how I functioned. I function because I have to, I function because I choose to; I function because I know nothing else. Or as Jennifer said, "You function because you are too competitive to let *them* win."

Jennifer makes me the proudest mother. She is somewhat of a spiritualist who takes comfort in the triumphant qualities of the human spirit. At 23, she has found a way to rid herself of the negative behaviors that once threatened to destroy her.

I wish that I had had her insight and fortitude at 23. But ah, regrets restrict real progress. I tell her everyday how much I love her. I hug her for no reason. I tell her how proud she makes me.

   She tried college but settle on being an entrepreneur. And by the way, traversing the Internet, Jennifer found Jerome with whom she isn't particularly fussed to forge a relationship. She says she was simply curious as to what he *sounded* like. I was upfront in letting him know his parental rights were legally terminated. He seemed shocked. He blames his mother for not relaying messages, for coming between him and his daughter. He is now living in North Carolina with his two children. His wife committed suicide on Father's Day 2012. His mother, Lee, died from breast cancer. His brother John lives is institutionalized.

   Then on May 27, 2013, while I was in Jamaica visiting my grandmother, I received a frantic call from Jennifer. Jerome was dead. Apparently, upon getting the call from Jerome's daughter, Jennifer simply said, "Now I'll never know what it's like to hug my father." Jen and I drove from Miami to North Carolina so she could at least 'see' Jerome. And see him she did, as we entered the funeral home, there he was lying in wait, demanding all attention. It was simply not possible to avert our eyes, as I had promised to never again view another lifeless body. Jen broke down. It was her first and last image of her father. She took the podium to tell him and everyone that she had forgiven his abandonment, and with complete resolute confidence, assured her new found siblings she would do for them what her father had failed to do for her: be there.

My Syd is now 17 and has already completed her freshman year at university where she's majoring in Philosophy and English. She's 5'11" and though I want her to pursue modeling, quite frankly she prefers academia. She is a brilliant writer, yea, I said it, and was voted most likely to receive the Pulitzer Prize. She has put off shuttling between living in Australia and America but visits Matt for a month every year. I'm grateful she has been spared the burdens of molestation and incest; I'm grateful she has not had to deal with the ravages that come from such interruptions.

As for as 'my three dads,' in my mind Mumfort is dead, I await the news of his physical death. With death comes finality, a burial of hope, of wishes. Bundy died, and it was fine, really. With his death came the end of an expectation that he might one day grow into a man and at least attempt reconciliation, to do for my children what he hadn't done for me. I wait for *that* finality with Mumfort, an end that would simply relieve him.

Claude has brought me my own joy and stability; a certain balance that says that marriage is not synonymous with care, with love, with empathy. I've been twice married and twice divorced. I now live in a happy state, free from talks of marriage, and really, that's just fine. He tells me everyday, how beautiful I am. He tells me how much he loves me—sometimes ten times a day. His support is total and far reaching. Yes, I found love when I was not even looking.

My Aunt Winsome has become one of the biggest advocates for us—helping each to heal in her own way, and in her own time. She leads, with total conviction, the cause for us to be made whole, and through her, I have found the courage and the determination to live a live free from the shackles of shame. She is my rock, my beacon, my mentor, my role model.

What I so crave now is some sort of assurance that that which afflicted my uncles and even some cousins, is in no way hereditary. I must confess I have tried to find empirical evidence to the contrary and remain terrified that maybe, just maybe it is a sickness passed down through generations.

But I cannot live on conjectures and theories. Nor can I spend the rest of my life wondering why they did what they did; that would be too much energy spent in vain. I now own, that while I am a sum of my experiences, a product of my circumstances, I am still and forever will be a result of an altered life, a path intersected, a person interrupted, a soul molested. And I'm okay with that because I'm okay with *me*. Though at times I had felt like selling hope, giving it to the highest bidder, I have finally learned to see the upside in everything, well most of the times. I have learned to appreciate the dark, without which light would have nothing to illuminate; I've learned to love the rain, without which the sun would be superfluous. I've learned to love even the pain, without which ease would cease to caress. I've learned to love the tears without which laughter would be monotone. And I've learned to love my experiences, all of them. I will not trade them; they've been such an intimate part of me that have actually become me. They have always been there, constant companion, on a journey that has led me to where I now love me! I love me—all of me.

That is not to say everything is *always* roses and wine. I sometimes mourn what I might have been had I been left to my own, had I not been fucked with. Then I remind myself that I cannot mourn that which I did not know, though I swear sometimes that is just a useless thing I tell myself when I want to escape the morose, and that mourning what I might have been is no different from mourning Michael Jackson or Whitney Houston; I only knew *of* them yet I mourned them. And then one of my therapists at the Journey Institute takes over my brain and keeps telling me, in answer to my ever present question: "what could I have been had I not been fucked with?" Her response soothes: look what you are *despite* being fucked with. Comforting. It is almost as comforting as what another therapist told me. She, barely into her thirties but with a wisdom reserved for the Platos of this world, had counseled that to people with unsolicited and unwelcome advice, I simply say: "thank you for caring, fuck you for sharing."

It was at the Journey Institute that I learned to finally release, to decompress, to not let myself be obsessed with the what ifs and the whys. It was there that I truly learned I was not alone in my pain, and perhaps more important, men hurt too. Men, like 'M' who was forced to have sex with his grandmother almost daily, and like 'T' who was repeatedly raped by his commanding officer back in Vietnam. Consciously or subconsciously, I no longer hated men; I saw that they too were victims—not just perpetrators. I became an empathizer.

I still can't empathize with my uncles though; too soon you could say. At the same time, I no longer obsess about revenge; it's simply too narrow a focus, too selfish. Instead, I pray for change. And I look to the day, when, behind the tourist veil of my beloved Jamaica, young girls—and boys—can be free to be, just be.

⌁

This you simply won't believe. On the afternoon of June 17, 2013, Syd dropped the biggest shock of my life: she too was violated—twice. This, I need to digest.

✞ ✞ ✞

Verily, verily I say unto thee, we speak that we do know, And testify that we have seen; and Ye receive not our witness.

—John 3:11

24735044R00198

Made in the USA
Charleston, SC
05 December 2013